Physician Employment Contracts

The Missing Module

A comprehensive introduction to physician agreements written for doctors

Elizabeth Shubov, JD

Advocate Press
Los Angeles, California
(213) 537-9905

Law Office of Elizabeth Shubov
433 N. Camden Drive, Suite 600
Beverly Hills, CA 90210
(310) 945-7381

ISBN-13 978-1-7337658-0-0

Dedication

This book is dedicated to my family and all of my clients who have shared their journeys and taught me so much over the years.

TABLE OF CONTENTS

DISCLAIMER

This book was written for educational purposes only. Reading this book does not create an attorney/client relationship. The information in this book is not legal advice and should not be considered legal advice as to any specific situation. It is always advisable to seek the help of an experienced attorney for a specific contract. Although the author has made every effort to ensure the information in this book was accurate at the time it was first published, the author does not assume and hereby disclaims any liability to any party for any loss, damage, or disruption caused by errors or omissions, whether such errors or omissions result from negligence, accident, or any other cause.

Preface

The majority of American medical schools do not provide any formal education with regard to signing a contract to provide medical services. Despite the lengthy medical training process, the skills and language required for physicians to protect themselves legally while practicing medicine are not incorporated into the curriculum. As a result, physicians graduate unprepared to evaluate employment contracts upon entering the workforce.

In the past, business and negotiation skills were sometimes transferred from one doctor to another in mentor relationships. Over the last few decades, shifts in the practice of medicine away from private practice and toward larger groups and hospital employment have meant fewer doctors receive this direct mentoring. Meanwhile, no formal channel has been developed for physicians to obtain a basic education in contractual relationships.

Physicians are often leery when it comes to negotiating and discussing legal issues because they are afraid it will appear as though they do not trust the hiring physicians. Hiring physicians suffer from the same lack of education and generally either take a very relaxed attitude toward contracts or go overboard trying to protect their interests. Non-physician administrators, business-minded individuals, and attorneys tasked with drafting agreements do not always understand the intricacies of the practice of medicine and draft contracts in a way that can be detrimental to a physician's right to practice and run afoul of anti-fraud laws. These administrators rarely have lawyers on their team or directly available, which leads to contracts that fail to protect a physician's interests. This confluence of factors often creates tensions as the parties negotiate important clauses in a contract.

The lack of emphasis on the importance of contracts and the hierarchical culture in medicine leads many physicians to sign their contracts blindly and not think about the consequences. Physicians that do advocate for themselves in contract negotiations sometimes run the risk of overstepping their boundaries or being labeled a "squeaky wheel." Even at large institutions, physicians can be strongly discouraged from requesting changes in a contract. It is perhaps most puzzling that when a specialty requires a physician to be meticulous and detail oriented, their loyalty and trust is questioned when they ask for reasonable changes to their agreements.

After many years as an attorney specializing in reviewing physician contracts, it has become clear that a resource is needed for physicians to obtain a basic education in the language of the agreements they are asked to sign. Physicians must be educated about what needs to be in their contracts and hiring physicians need to have the resources to provide appropriate and complete agreements to their new hires.

This book aims to empower physicians to feel confident and knowledgeable during contract negotiation and will help physicians learn about some common areas that often need to be carefully reviewed or restructured in a contract.

PART ONE

1. Introduction

It is crucial for a physician to ensure they have a complete and fair contract before signing. Signing a bad contract could have serious ramifications for a physician at any stage of practice. This book aims to help doctors understand some key contracting concepts to facilitate conversations and spot potential red flags in agreements. In this book, common clauses in physician contracts, contract structure, and specific clauses that require careful review in any agreement will be discussed.

This book will examine many of the common pitfalls in physician contracts including:

- missing, incomplete, or inaccurate basic terms;
- inadequate malpractice or "tail" coverage;
- invalid or overreaching non-competition agreements;
- inadequate or insufficient compensation arrangements;
- failure to comply with anti-fraud laws of importance in physician contracts;
- lack of specificity of location of service;
- balance of power issues; and
- waiver of important rights.

This book will also discuss effective strategies for negotiation, and a sample process for negotiating a contract. The last two sections of the book will discuss key clauses in physician contracts and special contracting situations as noted below.

Please refer to the full disclaimer at the beginning of this book. The information in this book should not be considered legal advice as to any specific situation. State laws vary, and it is not possible to cover every single issue or problem that can arise in a contract. It is always advisable to seek the help of an experienced attorney for a specific contract.

How to Read and Use this Book

Sections of this book will need to be read more than once to absorb all of the information. Many of the topics discussed will become clearer when applied to an actual contract and circumstance. This book will primarily focus on employment and independent contractor relationships with groups and hospitals although it will touch on other agreements as well. Throughout the book, California law is referenced by way of example to explain complex contracting clauses and concepts. The reader should be aware that laws do vary state to state. However, the concepts are transferrable to contracts in most states.

There are references in the book to court cases, sections, and codes of law. Most of the laws referenced are complex, and this book attempts to summarize some of the relevant sections. The references are included for the reader's benefit, but please understand that many of these references may not be easily understood without a legal background. Just as with medical research, there is background language of the law that needs to be understood to interpret cases and statutes. This is another reason to seek the help of a professional for specific contractual issues.

This book has five sections to allow the reader to jump around and find the most pertinent information at any given time.

Part One discusses why a physician should thoroughly read his or her contract, and contains advice from the author about evaluating job prospects and planning for a long career in medicine.

Part Two discusses types of contracts, compensation, benefits, Fair Market Value, and negotiation.

Part Three provides a narrative of a sample hiring process, a short lesson in reading a contract, and a sample contract. This section is primarily for reference.

Part Four discusses many of the important clauses and concepts found in physician employment and contractor agreements in more detail, including Contract Term and Termination; Professional Liability and other Insurance; Restraints on Competition and Confidentiality; Intellectual Property; Integration; Arbitration and Dispute Resolution; Indemnity and "Hold Harmless" Clauses; Major Federal Anti-Fraud Laws; Hospital Privileges and Due Process; and other Miscellaneous Contract Provisions.

Part Five discusses some special contracting situations, including Recruitment Agreements, Ownership Agreements, Medical Directorships, and Academic Medicine Appointments.

Common Questions

Are contracts different from state to state?

Yes, many provisions in contracts are controlled by state law, and laws vary from one state to another. This book occasionally focuses on California law, although many of the concepts are applicable in other states.

Aren't all contracts standard with boilerplate language?

NO! If you take one thing away from this book, it should be that every contract is different and should be read on its merit. It is a common misconception that contracts are standardized. Before anything else, any new contract should be read cover to cover. Even within large institutions, there can be significant variations in contracts and a need for significant revisions. As large institutions acquire smaller practices, carefully reviewing contracts has become even more important. The contracts from large institutions right now seem to be less vetted by legal departments than in the past. One cannot assume anything is standard language to be glanced over without careful reading.

Are there some red flags to look for in a contract?

Many red flags will be discussed in this book. Ideally, a person without legal training should be able to read a contract and understand the basics terms of the new position. Basic terms include: whom the physician is working for, the compensation arrangement, the location of work, benefits, the length of the contract, and how the contract can terminate. There will certainly be some legalese that will be difficult to understand, but if the basic terms are not clear from looking at a contract, then there is a problem with the contract. If there is a lot of language that would make the average person roll their eyes, for example, "This contract will be valid throughout the whole universe…" one should question whether it is a well drafted or well-tailored agreement. Believe it or not, that is a direct quote from a physician contract.

I was told this is the contract everyone signed so it should be fine, right?

Not necessarily. A physician could receive an objectively terrible or one-sided contract that many other doctors have signed without reading. Well-drafted contracts are the exception rather than the norm. It doesn't matter if the contracts come from large institutions, small private practices, or regional hospitals. Spelling errors, missing information, and contracts that are outright copied from other organizations and not tailored to a particular position are common. Remember, many doctors don't read their contracts. Select, well-integrated health systems have crafted their contracts to the point where that health system can be said to have a somewhat "standard" contract. But even within these institutions, there is variation. Human Resources departments will cut corners and take a contract drafted for another purpose and re-purpose it without ever contacting the legal department. It is vitally important that a physician is always their own advocate and not assume anything is standardized.

How is this different from entering into a contract during training?

The hierarchy of training asks physicians to fall in line and trust their elders. Most trainees do not read any of their training contracts. Due to the set-up of the resident contracting system, if they wanted to train, they had to sign. In training institutions, all parties have an interest in protecting the trainees under an academic umbrella. It is almost a parental relationship that training institutions have with their trainees.

When contracting to provide medical services as an attending physician or surgeon, employers or future colleagues are no longer guaranteed to be looking out for an individual doctor's best interests. They are contracting with a doctor to provide a service and therefore are looking to protect themselves and the finances of the practice or hospital. Doctors need to be aware of their vulnerabilities out of training, learn to be their own advocates, and not put too much trust in the hiring physicians. Trainees often graduate with some version of an inferiority complex about their level of experience and worth as a fully credentialed doctor. After all of your training, don't let a bad contract hurt your future as a doctor. Take note of whatever baggage you may have from training, but don't let it deter you from negotiating the position and respect you deserve.

Who should REALLY consult an attorney about their contract?

As an attorney, I recommend having all contracts reviewed by a professional before signing. However, this is a little like telling everyone they have to go for their annual check-up with their PCP; it is unlikely to happen. The following are some situations in which you are more likely to need the help of an attorney and in some instances, an accountant.

- Community/Regional Hospital Contracts: Even large institutions have trouble producing compliant physician contracts. Smaller hospitals and regional medical centers often have less access to legal counsel and therefore do not produce contracts that are complete and ready for signature. This is a generalization and unfortunately does not mean one can rest easy at a larger institution. Pay particularly close attention when contracting with a community or regional hospital.

- Joining a Group Practice: Group practices are businesses, and there are no standards in this business for physician contracts.

There are many details necessary for a group practice contract, and very often they are left out either because of a lack of knowledge or careless errors in the agreement. Sometimes there are perceived "unspoken agreements" or verbal understandings that are not sufficient to protect the physician. Physicians should make sure they have fair representation in a group agreement and that the work, liabilities, and revenue are shared in an equitable fashion.

- Shareholder/Partnership Agreements: Shareholder and Partnership agreements come in a lot of different forms. Promises made are not always memorialized in a contract and can lead to problems down the line.

- Recruitment/Relocation/Guaranteed Income Agreements: These arrangements are complicated and often include a secured loan of a large sum of money as a guaranteed income for the first year. For these contracts, I recommend not only the assistance of an attorney but also an accountant to help navigate the liabilities and risks involved.

- Intellectual Property Rights: I practice in California where it seems everyone gets involved or enticed by the promise of getting rich or changing the world through technological inventions at some point. A physician inclined toward research, inventions, patenting, etc., may require intellectual property protection and should thoroughly vet these sections of any contract. Most contracts will demand ownership over inventions or intellectual property produced in any way with the employer's time or materials.

- Administrative portions of position: If a physician is a medical director, hires other doctors, manages QI (Quality Improvement) programs, oversees advanced practice providers, or any other administrative duties as part of the position, then the contract may warrant further review. These types of administrative duties are subject to special care for Fair Market Value (FMV) determinations.

What do I do if I have a problem with a current contract?

If you are currently under contract, the best thing to do is seek the advice of an employment law attorney to analyze options moving forward. This book will provide guidance as to the meaning of many sections of contracts. However, each contract is unique, and as such, it would be advantageous to speak with someone directly who can help determine rights and options under a current agreement.

2. Choosing the Right Job

Make a plan for your career. If a doctor wants to have a long career in medicine, they should take some time for self-reflection and do so often. Physicians need to find jobs that are right for them, not just ones that meet certain monetary, scheduling, or locational criteria. A lot of physicians end up caught on the treadmill of productivity and forget their long-term career or lifestyle goals. Goals and motivations can also change over time. With every new contract, it is necessary to analyze all aspects of the position keeping in mind the goals, needs, and wants of the individual doctor. This is especially important for a doctor that is not happy in their current position and feels "under the gun" to make a significant change. Rushing to accept a job can be one of the biggest mistakes a doctor can make in their career and often facilitates physician burnout.

Younger physicians are often anxious to accept the first position that meets whatever they see as their most important requirements whether location, salary, work schedule, or perhaps a chance to work with a mentor. More experienced physicians may find themselves in a lousy work environment, full of emotions and interpersonal issues and be eager to make a quick change. In all situations, it is advisable to take a step back and evaluate all prospects holistically.

This book will discuss many red flags physicians should look out for when contracting for a new position. One of the most important predictors for the longevity of a relationship is the balance of power in the negotiating process and how that may affect the relationship between the parties and the future work environment. If the doctors and administrators are contentious during the contracting process, this can be a red flag that the future working relationship may not be smooth sailing. If the contracting process makes it clear a physician will have no power in the working relationship, one can imagine what will happen when any issues or problems arise later. For this reason, a challenging contract negotiation process may be of great potential benefit to the prospective employee who may recognize a bad situation before becoming bound to it.

Location, Location, Location! The old real estate adage holds true in life. The location of a new position is an essential consideration. Many physicians are drawn toward remote areas with promises of high pay and extensive leisure time. It is understood in the medical profession, that if you want to make more money, you have to go outside of the city to an underserved area. While there are many reasons to move to underserved areas, money should not be the primary motivator. Yes, the cost of living is lower, and good doctors are needed in more remote and underserved areas. In recent years, however, some major cities have become much more competitive. As we will discuss in Chapter 4, when evaluating a position, one should always factor in all forms of compensation and benefits when comparing salaries. Many doctors are shocked that they can stay at academic centers in California and do quite well or go to private hospitals in urban areas and make a similar income as they would expect in a remote, underserved area.

Jobs in medicine are not one size fits all. Some people will be more satisfied and comfortable in a very high productivity private practice with a lot of opportunities to make money. Others may feel better in a large health system where they only have to worry about seeing patients and documenting their patient visits. All options come with pros and cons. It is important to not put yourself in the position you think you should be in, but rather a position that you will thrive in and have a long, productive medical career.

PART TWO

3. Types and Format of Contracts

Contracts come in all forms, from a handshake at the end of a conversation to something written on the back of a bar napkin to an iTunes licensing agreement. This chapter will briefly look at some of the most common types of contracts for physicians and why it is so important to read them thoroughly.

A contract is an agreement between parties creating mutual obligations enforceable by law.[1] An employment contract lays out the duties and responsibilities of each party and the wages and benefits that will be provided in exchange for the work. A contract is legally binding whether it is written or oral, though you will see why it is imperative for a physician to have a written agreement as you read through this book.

The consequences of breaking a contract are sometimes spelled out in the agreement. If the employer or contractor brings a physician to court or arbitration for breaking a contract, damages will be calculated.[2] The calculation of damages can include a range of considerations but will undoubtedly cover costs associated with the departure and finding a replacement physician. If a physician is considering breaking a contract, it is best to speak to an employment lawyer before taking any affirmative steps to leave the position.

Contract Format

There are no standards in physician contracts. Some contracts have bullet points and neat headings, while others are written in long paragraphs. Some universities or large health systems will provide a two-page offer letter and a pile of manuals instead of a full-length contract. The appearance of the contract does not indicate how well or poorly it is drafted. Some contracts are laid out perfectly and are terrible contracts, while others are numbered with no headings and long paragraphs and contain the necessary elements. Physicians often see block language in contracts and assume it is "boilerplate" language. Boilerplate is a term that comes from an old method of printing and is used to describe language that is considered standard and often cannot be negotiated.[3] In my experience, with few exceptions, boilerplate language does not exist in physician contracts. Instead, in my opinion, terms alluding to the standardization of contracts are often used to disempower the physician from participating in the negotiation process.

It is common to see a contract from another industry modified into a contract for a physician to provide medical services. These contracts are often dangerously incomplete or contain terms that if a physician is held to could have significant impacts on the physician's career practicing medicine. I cannot stress enough how important it is to have such a contract reviewed and amended to comply with some of the legal intricacies of physician contracting.

Letter of Understanding

A letter of understanding (LOU) is a one to five-page document that details all of the basic terms agreed upon by the physician and employer before a formal contract is drawn up for signature. The idea of an LOU can be confusing because it may state across the top of the document that the LOU is "non-binding on either party." This means that if a physician signs such a letter, they could decide to take a different position and abandon the terms of the LOU completely without suffering legal consequences. However, a physician should always be sure they agree with the contents of the LOU if they plan to take the position. In addition, it is important to make sure that everything in the LOU is documented in the final contract. The LOU will have no legal significance after a final contract is signed. A little later in the book, in Part Three, there is a narrative about a sample hiring process that will describe an LOU in action.

Employment Manuals and Exhibits

As a physician reads through their contract initially, they should make a note of any referenced documents. If the contract references manuals, make sure none of the manuals are missing, as essential information can be in these documents. It is ideal to get the full copy of the referenced document before signing the contract. Sometimes only part of a manual is disclosed because the organization wants to protect the proprietary nature of the documents. Referenced documents and attached exhibits should be considered part of the employment agreement, and one has a right to view them before signing. I have reviewed contracts where the "for cause" termination provisions were in a manual and it was challenging to obtain copies of the documents. These are important terms. If it is referenced in the contract, it is part of the contract, and you have a right to see it.

Types of Contracts

Employment Agreements

An employment agreement sets out the rights, expectations, obligations, and restrictions of a working relationship. An employee receives a W-2 at the end of the year, taxes are paid by the employer, and hopefully, the employer will provide an array of benefits such as health insurance and professional liability coverage. An employer may have some degree of control over the tasks performed at work and the right to restrict the physician's ability to practice medicine outside of the employer's practice/hospital.[4] A proper employment agreement can offer some safe harbor protections from anti-fraud laws which will be discussed in Chapter 17.

Independent Contractor Agreements

An independent contractor agreement sets out the agreed upon terms and responsibilities of both parties. An independent contractor receives a 1099 at the end of the year and is required to pay his/her taxes.[5] Technically, a physician should not be hired as an independent contractor unless they have complete control over their work and time.[6] However, in some states physicians have traditionally been hired as independent contractors for legal reasons. The section below on the corporate practice of medicine doctrine explains why physicians traditionally could not be employed directly by hospitals or groups in some states and how groups and hospitals can now employ physicians in some cases.

As independent contractors, physicians may set up a corporation through which they can pay all expenses, taxes, and a salary for themselves. The requirements and structure for corporations that provide medical services vary by state. California only allows professionals to incorporate as a professional corporation (PC) and not as a limited liability company (LLC) or other business entity type.[7]

It is essential to review independent contractor agreements thoroughly, as they can leave physicians open to unintended liability if they do not comply with the strict criteria for safe harbors and exceptions under certain anti-fraud laws. Independent contractors also need to review indemnity clauses carefully and should factor in expenses such as benefits and professional liability insurance when comparing offers.

Partnership Agreements

A partnership agreement is a contract between two or more physicians that is used to establish the responsibilities of each partner and how the practice will collectively be governed.[8] Profits and liabilities are shared among the parties involved according to terms of the agreement.[9]

Shareholder/Ownership Agreement

A shareholder agreement will often start as an employment agreement with a "buy-in" option to become a shareholder of the medical practice or group. Shareholder status will then be offered or not offered by the employer at a later date. Chapter 21 will discuss Shareholder Agreements later on in the book.

Locum Tenens

Locum Tenens contracts are temporary appointments, where a physician is filling the shoes of another doctor for a short amount of time.[10] These appointments are heavily regulated and usually filled by Locum Agencies. It is important to read the contracts, and despite what many people have heard, these agreements are often quite negotiable.

"We don't have contracts" Contract

"There is no contract" or "We don't have contracts," is something I hear more and more. If you are asked to sign a letter of understanding or offer letter that is only two pages long and given a stack of sixty pages of documents containing an intellectual property agreement, non-disclosure agreement, arbitration agreement, due process clauses, etc., consider this all your contract. In my opinion, the language stating "we do not have contracts" is said to make the contract seem less negotiable and less important. A physician should always remember that their license is on the line, and a medical license is what allows one to work as a physician and enables the institution hiring the physician to get paid. Do not believe a contract is only two pages long, especially when working for a large institution or practice.

Corporate Practice of Medicine Doctrine

Let's say you've been offered a job at a hospital, but when you receive your contract, it is from a medical group, not the hospital. Why does this happen? California, like many states, has a corporate practice of medicine doctrine. The Medical Practice Act in the California Business and Professions Code prohibits any person from practicing medicine in the state without a valid license.[11] As such, "Corporations and other artificial entities shall have no professional rights, privileges, or powers."[12] This means that a hospital cannot directly hire physicians because the corporate entity is not licensed to practice medicine and therefore cannot oversee the practice.

The prohibition against the corporate practice of medicine in states with such a doctrine is meant to protect patients from untrained persons or heads of entities making or influencing a physician's professional judgment or interfering with medical decisions. It also reduces the chances of divided loyalties between physician and employer and physician and patient. Physicians are highly trained and should be able to practice their profession freely, in the best interests of their patients, free from pressure from an employer or special interest. The physician must control the medical aspects of the practice and their relationship with their patients.[13]

There are exceptions to this doctrine in California, specified by statute if certain conditions are met, which include charitable institutions, medical foundations, academic institutions, teaching hospitals, and clinics.[14] Many groups and hospitals have established foundations that are controlled by physicians and are charged with overseeing and maintaining the medical staff of the hospital. If the physicians hire and have control over the medical staff, there is no longer a corporate practice of medicine issue. In Chapter 8, "How to Read a Contract," we will discuss some of the implications of this doctrine and how it changes the structure of employment for physicians in states with similar doctrines.

4. Compensation and Benefits

The amount of compensation for a new position is often among the first concerns of a physician when entertaining a new offer. For young physicians, it may be the first time after nearly two decades of school and training that they will receive a "real" salary. The most important thing to remember about this topic area is to look at the compensation as a whole, including benefits, not just the dollar amount of the pay. Physicians can become fixated on the salary number, thinking it is not high enough when the total compensation is in a perfect range. On the other end of the spectrum, salaries that are beyond Fair Market Value are subject to their own legal scrutiny. When determining appropriate compensation, it is important to look at individual training and experience and begin to figure out what is considered Fair Market Value for a given position. Fair Market Value will be discussed in more detail in the next chapter.

This chapter will also discuss benefits and bonuses. These items must be factored into total compensation and are often easier to negotiate than base salary. Larger institutions may have a very strict organizational rubric to follow for salary, but benefits are generally a little more flexible.

Compensation Arrangement

A compensation arrangement should detail the structure of payments for providing medical services and is one of the most critical parts of a contract. Surprisingly, this section of an agreement often lacks crucial details. Every contract should explain how pay will be calculated. There does not need to be a hard number of how much a physician will be paid each year, but there should be a formula for determining overall compensation. Compensation schemes can get quite complicated, and the contract represents an opportunity for transparency and clarity to ensure that the physician is compensated appropriately for their work.

Some contracts "incorporate in by reference" attachments for compensation arrangements, employment manuals, and other documents. Details of compensation and benefits may be written into the contract or attached as an addendum/exhibit but must be readily available and certain. In these cases, it is imperative that the attachments and manuals be included in the packet for the physician's review of the full contract. All documents must be part of or referenced in the final contract to be considered part of the final agreement. This is called "integration," and it will be discussed in Chapter 14 of this book.

Shifting to Quality-Based Incentive Compensation

The current trend in the medical community is to move from production-based compensation systems to quality-based incentives and pay.[15] This is happening for a number of reasons including changes to federal programs such as the 2015 passage of Medicare Access and Reauthorization Act (MACRA), which includes an option for merit-based incentive payment systems (MIPS).[16] Some institutions are instituting incentive pay systems and paying physicians based on patient panel size, quality metrics, and other non-traditional or nonproduction-based metrics. The goal is to incorporate meaningful performance metrics to facilitate behavioral changes among providers in an attempt to improve care, outcomes, reduce provider burnout, and maximize dollars in the practice and hospital settings.

Doctors, groups, and hospital systems must take into account these changes and shifts when determining appropriate compensation metrics for a new position. Most groups and hospitals that are shifting payment structures are doing so gradually and mixing quality incentives with RVUs or other production-based methods.[17] In addition, physicians taking on leadership roles within organizations present special challenges and large hospital systems buying smaller practices often keep in place the compensation schemes of those practices. This results in misaligned payments where a physician in the same specialty in the same system can make dramatically different wages.

Stacking Arrangements

Stacking arrangements occur when a physician is hired for more than one position and pose challenges when looking at the Fair Market Value of the agreement.[18] For compensation purposes, "stacking" refers to paying a physician for different positions they hold, for work they may be doing simultaneously. If a physician is a medical director and internist, they may have two different contracts, with two different compensation arrangements. To evaluate the compensation under this circumstance, one must figure out how often/for how many hours they will perform each position and look at the compensation and benefits through the lens of those details.

Bonus Arrangements

Sign-on bonuses, retention, quality incentives, and productivity bonuses are common in physician contracts. Bonus arrangements must be detailed in the contract and not leave too much at the sole discretion of the employer. As is the case with other forms of compensation, there must be a formula for determining bonuses.[19] If a bonus arrangement is too vague, it could raise speculation of fraud in the contract. A physician should make sure they completely understand what kinds of bonuses are contained in the contract and any responsibilities attached to bonuses, including when a physician may be required to pay them back. Examples of bonuses that may need to be repaid are retention bonuses or sign-on bonuses if the physician does not stay for the required amount of time or meet the conditions of the original payment.

Relocation and Moving Expenses

Relocation and moving expenses are often offered by an organization to entice a physician to move for a new position. There are generally specific requirements that need to be met for reimbursement and physicians need to beware of any conditions that may trigger a responsibility to repay this money. Just as with bonuses, if a physician does not stay with the practice for a certain amount of time, they may be liable to pay back some or all of the money received.

Benefits

If a physician has a family and kids, they no doubt have come to understand the importance of good health insurance, retirement packages, and paid time off. Sometimes physicians think that it shows poor work ethic to ask about such benefits. On the contrary, benefits are a very important part of what will or will not make a position sustainable for a physician and their family. Benefits are meant to entice a physician to work for and stay with a certain hospital or practice. It is well within the physician's rights to ask about all benefits of the position and inquire about other benefits needed to make the position sustainable.

Benefits that may be included in a compensation package include but are not limited to: incentive pay programs, relocation expenses, health and dental insurance, professional liability insurance, paid vacation and sick time, life insurance, disability insurance, student loan payments, medical staff dues, professional dues, licensing fees, attorney fees, business expenses, leave of absence, severance pay, CME, pension, disability/pregnancy leave, and sabbatical.

Parental Leave and Sabbatical

Many young doctors are afraid if they ask about maternity and paternity leave, they will not get hired. My response to these individuals is always that they are no longer in training. Physicians need to not only make money in this new position but enjoy their lives for it to be a sustainable career. Many employers, when hiring a young physician, are expecting such questions or are anticipating that the physician may need to take leave at some point. Keep in mind that if questions about benefits are met with hostility, this is an important piece of information regarding the work environment that may help in the decision-making process. If an employer is shocked by a young doctor asking about maternity or paternity benefits, it may not be the job for them if they are planning to have a family and a balanced life.

In addition to parental leave benefits, though rare, there are some groups and academic centers that allow for a traditional sabbatical whether for extended vacation or advancement of academic pursuits. The terms of these sabbaticals are specific to each organization and can be a nice benefit option.

Paid Time Off, Vacation, and Sick Time

Employers have some leeway with how they provide paid time off of work. They can provide "Paid Time Off (PTO)" and include all vacation time, sick time, and CME time in one pool of time or each area can be designated separately. I often see contracts that state if a physician does not use their vacation time by the end of the year, it will be lost. State laws vary, but in California, a "use or lose it" vacation or paid time off policy is not legal.[20] Generally, if paid time off is earned, then it cannot be taken away and must be paid out at the end of employment.[21] In California, vacation days can cap out at a certain number of weeks so that a physician can no longer accrue beyond a certain number of days until they start using them. This type of policy is valid and different from "use-it-or-lose-it" because the vacation days are not being taken away.

Insurance Coverage

Insurance coverage can be a significant benefit to employment. Not only malpractice but also general commercial liability, errors and omissions, directors and officers, and possibly medical director coverage can all be important considerations. Please see Chapter 11 for a more in-depth discussion on insurance.

Call Coverage

State law and individual group and practice policies on separate compensation for call coverage vary quite a bit. Whether or not a physician is compensated for call sometimes hinges on whether the call is voluntary or mandatory. It also depends on if the physician is being compensated for the call in some other way in their compensation package. It is best for a physician to familiarize themselves with the community standards and state law to determine if they should seek compensation for call coverage.

Supervising Advanced Practice Clinicians (APC)

It is common to take on supervisory duties as a physician; supervising other practitioners such as Nurse Practitioners, Physician Assistants, trainees, allied health professionals, etc. When a physician does this, they are taking on a certain amount of liability in supervising the providers and also some extra work. Many positions will compensate supervision in some manner, whether on a flat fee per provider, a fee for a capped number of providers, a percentage of the generated RVUs or a combination of RVUs and cost of the practitioner. Look at the supervisory duties, how much extra work it entails, and overall pay structure to determine if there should be extra compensation available for supervising APCs. Make sure payments are not being stacked for APCs as it could run afoul of Fair Market Value determinations. Not all health systems and practices compensate separately for supervising APCs, but it is worth asking the extent of one's role and if there will be separate compensation.

Independent Contractor Agreements "1099"

Independent Contractors technically work independently from their employer, without benefits, and are paid without taxes withheld.[22] When someone says they are paid 1099, it means he or she will be responsible for paying all of his or her taxes and must secure his or her own benefits. This often presents as a larger paycheck upfront, so it is tempting to look at independent contractor positions and think that the overall compensation is higher than an employment agreement. However, when the amount paid in taxes, benefits, and malpractice is factored in, the advantage is often illusory.

Malpractice insurance is an important consideration with independent contractor agreements. Some independent contractor physicians negotiate with the hiring organization to cover professional liability insurance. This is purely a matter of contract. If a physician is working for a group, they can request the group cover the policy or reimburse the cost of an individual policy. On a private plan, a physician will almost certainly need to purchase their own tail insurance after employment, which will be another significant added expense. Please see Chapter 11 on "Professional Liability and Insurance" for more information on insurance.

Review of Benefits

Make sure to review these and all other benefits carefully. A list of questions one may want to ask a future employer include:

- How many vacation days will I receive?
- Will there be paid CME time with reimbursement for costs?
- Will I be reimbursed for license renewal, DEA renewal, and professional fees?
- Is there any assistance with student loan payments?
- Will I have paid administrative time?
- What type of retirement plans are available?
- What type of health insurance benefits are available for myself and my family?
- Are there Health Savings Accounts, Flexible Spending Accounts, or Dependent Care Funds available?
- Will malpractice coverage be provided and does it include "tail coverage?"

5. Fair Market Value

Compensation arrangements in contracts to provide medical services must be Fair Market Value (FMV) under anti-fraud laws including Stark Law and Anti-Kickback Statute (AKS).[23] Unfortunately, there are no hard and fast rules about how to figure out what is and what is not FMV. According to commentary on Stark Law, to show FMV, there must be evidence that the compensation is comparable to what is ordinarily paid for an item or service in the location at issue and one must be able to explain and defend the compensation scheme in any contract.[24]

Essentially, if overall compensation is considered too high or too low for an individual in a given specialty, it can create an appearance of possible fraudulent activity. As such, it is up to the physician to determine if they are being compensated for more than the work performed. If so, they should carefully consider if there could be a problem with the extra payments. Physicians paid at the level of a clinical physician for doing work that could be done by someone else for significantly lower pay may also raise red flags.

There are various tests and valuation methods used in the industry to determine FMV that should be considered in any analysis including the Fair Market Value Standard, the Commercial Reasonableness Standard, and determining if the contract takes into account referrals for designated health services (DHS).[25] We will discuss the anti-fraud laws such as Stark Law, AKS, and others in Chapter 17 and get into the specifics of referrals for DHS at that time.

The Fair Market Value (FMV) Standard

Under the FMV Standard,[26] the aggregate compensation paid to a physician over the term of the agreement must be:

1. Set in advance;
2. Consistent with Fair Market Value in an arms-length transaction; and
3. Not determined in a manner that takes into account the volume or value of any referrals or business otherwise generated between the parties.

This requirement that compensation must be set in advance means it must follow a set formula. A physician does not necessarily have to be able to calculate the total amount of compensation they will receive at the end of the year, but it must be clear if one works X amount and bills Y procedures that they will make Z money at the end of the year. This rule applies to bonus payments as well. There must be defined terms for a bonus, such that it is not just in the employer's sole discretion.

There are many different metrics used by experts to determine FMV. The most widely used is survey data which is discussed below.

The requirement that the transaction must be arms-length means it should be one in which both parties have relatively equal leverage and are both interested in making a deal.[27]

Finally, a common theme under most anti-fraud rules relevant to physicians is that physicians cannot be paid to send referrals for services covered under federal Medicare or Medicaid programs, except under certain circumstances. Physicians must be independent in their medical judgment and free to refer to where they believe best for the patient.[28] The physician cannot be paid to generate business for the practice outside of their capacity as a physician seeing their patients. This will be discussed further in Chapter 17 on "Anti-Fraud Laws."

Commercial Reasonableness Standard

The commercial reasonableness test says an arrangement must be analyzed as a sensible, prudent business arrangement to be valid even in the absence of any fraudulent activity.[29] The test is important as it recognizes that if a doctor is hired for a position where a doctor is not needed, it may raise red flags for fraud regulators. It would not be reasonable to hire a doctor for a position where a doctor is not required and certainly not reasonable to pay a doctor's salary when someone else could do the job for much lower pay. If individual compensation is very high, it may not be commercially reasonable to hire a specific physician unless it is shown that the person is uniquely qualified to perform the services for more money.

The two questions that should be asked in any situation are:

1. Is a doctor required?
2. Is a doctor of this skill level required?

Reliability of Survey Compensation Data

There are many annual surveys and consulting firms that aggregate physician compensation data. Physicians often ask about Medical Group Management Association (MGMA), American Medical Group Association (AMGA), and other survey data and if they can use it to determine if they are receiving a reasonable offer and are within FMV. The organizations synthesize an enormous amount of data, and consequentially the data is often portrayed as an accurate hardline representation of the salaries of all physicians across the country. Depending on the position, these data sets can be helpful, but they should not be relied on as the sole determining factor of FMV.

Since there is no mandate to report data to these organizations, there are higher concentrations of certain types of positions and the data is not precisely reflective of the market. The surveys are weighted more heavily in specialties and specific geographic areas where they have more respondents.[30] Some companies will publish the number of venues associated with each of their data sets so one can get a little more of an idea of the weight and size of the organizations participating. This is helpful, but this data is still not determinative for what is a "good offer" at any given time.

Some survey organizations allow a free trial on their website to pull the data or pay for prepared reports to get a general idea of median compensation for a given specialty. Keep in mind that the market might be performing quite differently at any given time. If you look at scatterplots, the data is varied, and there are a lot of factors to be taken into account such as RVUs, quality incentive payments, commercial payor rates, payer mix, service mix (ancillaries, call services, admin, nonproduction services), profits for non-physician providers, and cost efficiency.

Use caution not to confuse total compensation with base compensation in the data and don't try to match percentile benchmarks and productivity benchmarks. Multiple factors affect physician compensation and the economics of physician practices, not just RVUs. If a physician has a guaranteed income contract for a set number of years or a recruitment agreement, the starting salary may not be within FMV and may not match the data. Stacking arrangements where a physician is being hired for multiple positions under the same or different contracts require special attention for FMV determination and may make looking at survey data difficult.

Data Sets and Fair Market Value

Valuation experts often say that 50th percentile to 75th percentile is Fair Market Value within a given specialty and geographic area.[31] These numbers do not provide a concrete rule and don't have any codification that I can find. It is simply—"how everyone does it." According to the IRS, valuations are always based on facts and circumstances—there are no formulas.[32] If you have a position with a more defined rubric, using these scatterplots may be accurate. However, most jobs do not fit into a neat box and have many responsibilities and considerations that may be unique to an area or hospital system. Using multiple surveys and using the median, instead of the mean, as the central point in data, can produce a potentially more accurate estimate. Some of the definitions in different survey data can vary. Therefore, physicians should avoid making any assumptions about what they think they see in the data, and try to determine what each data set is actually showing.

Quality Incentive Payments and Fair Market Value

As groups and hospitals switch to using quality metrics instead of production-based metrics, use caution when looking at survey data. Surveys are often not precise enough to differentiate between organizations that have added quality metrics and incentives to their compensation packages and those who have not.

Resist the temptation to look at the median compensation on survey data and add in incentive pay. This practice can lead to an inaccurate analysis of FMV because a reporting organization may have already factored incentive pay into the data in the surveys.

Physicians Leadership Roles and Fair Market Value

Some significant issues arise when a physician leaves the practice of medicine to take on an administrative leadership role. Administrative and teaching roles are typically paid less than purely clinical work. Remember, all physician agreements must be commercially reasonable. Is it commercially reasonable to take a physician out of clinical practice and pay them much more than you would pay another administrator to do the same job? This question is coming up more and more and often the answer is often no; it is not reasonable to continue to pay a physician at the physician's prior salary level if they move into an administrative role. These situations require extra caution to ensure the physicians are not being overpaid in a way that could appear fraudulent.

Common Questions

Are there professionals that determine FMV?

One way to determine FMV for a position is to hire an independent valuation consultant to run the numbers and compare the pay and responsibilities to that of other similarly situated physicians according to industry benchmarks. Many companies offer this service; however, it is expensive to have such an analysis run on a specific contract. Often employers in large institutions will have a valuation report prepared for their files, and a physician can ask to view this document when considering a position. In the event of a high-value position with many moving parts, it may be worthwhile for the individual physician to take matters into their own hands and pay for a report.

What happens if I sign a contract that is paid above FMV?

In 2015, the Office of Inspector General (OIG) issued a fraud alert concerning physician compensation and specifically put physicians on notice that they need to be careful about the FMV of the contracts they are signing.[33] The OIG is a federal agency that distributes resources to the health care industry in an effort to assist compliance with fraud and abuse laws and to educate the public about fraudulent schemes. It is worth respecting their warnings.

Many of the fraud cases brought against groups, hospital systems, and individual physicians initiate as whistleblower actions, also known as Qui Tam lawsuits.[34] This happens when a person tips off regulators to abnormally high payments or potentially fraudulent situations. Other cases come about through routine audits or fraud task forces.[35] These claims, as well as actions of the OIG, are difficult to predict. The smartest thing to do is to consider FMV upfront when entering into any new contract.

Is there any way to be 100% sure that my contract is FMV?

Unfortunately, no. The best we can do is try to follow all of the guidance and take into account all payments and benefits received for employment.

6. Negotiation

Whether a doctor is negotiating their first contract or tenth, negotiation should be viewed simply as a strategic conversation with the future employer. At some stages of practice this conversation may take place in a boardroom accompanied by counsel, but most often it is accomplished by email, phone, and in-person meetings. Physicians usually negotiate directly with the hiring parties when the discussions are about terms that are within a physician's personal or professional zone of understanding, such as compensation, work hours, benefits, and schedule. For matters that are of legal significance, it is best to retain counsel to help ensure proper protection for the physician and proper drafting.

When does the negotiation begin?

Negotiation should start at some level from the very first conversation between the physician and hiring parties. The physician will want to make their needs and wants known to the employer when discussing and agreeing to the basic terms of the contract. Some tact should be used in deciding when to make specific requests depending on the nature of the relationship with the employer and timeline for interviews and hiring. In the next part of the book, we will look at some sample contract language and a sample hiring process. Each situation is unique, and it is important for the physician to "know their audience" so to speak when negotiating and making requests for changes to an offer or contract. An attorney can often help navigate this process, but the physician may be in the best position to determine from social cues and correspondence how to move forward with a negotiation.

How much leverage does a physician have?

Leverage depends on the specialty, type of contract, experience of the physician, market forces, availability of other physicians, and priorities of the hiring parties. Whether a physician is newly out of training or at the peak of their career, it is important to remember how much training has been completed and how valuable the skills are to an employer. It is always worth trying to negotiate for yourself. The extent to which one will ultimately decide to push a negotiation or demand specific terms as a condition of accepting a position will be different in every situation. Some terms such as relocation bonuses or student loan payments are "wants" but not necessarily "needs" of a physician. Other times there are legal issues in the contract such as an illegal non-compete clause that if not changed may ultimately end the conversation.

It is important to pick your battles and focus on the most critical items first. When a hospital system or employer is not accustomed to physicians thoroughly reviewing their contracts and advocating for themselves, even small undisputed changes can seem excessive. Requesting too many changes at once can lead to some pushback. Often if there is significant pushback about adding detail to a contract or changing the legal language, it is because the hiring physicians do not know what is in the contract and don't want to spend their time finding out. Other times, changes to the contract are avoided because it would require further involvement of a Human Resources department or other attorneys and can greatly slow down the hiring process. These issues have little to do with the prospective employee but should be recognized for what they are. Fear of administrative delays must be differentiated from attempts to strong-arm the physician into complying with certain terms.

Of course, many practices and groups prefer that physicians do not negotiate their agreements. Surprisingly, the groups that are often the worst about this tend to be in specialties that require the physicians to be assertive and detail-oriented professionally. When these same physicians want simple changes in their contracts, even for undisputed terms, it can be seen as too much detail, and the prospective hire is made to feel like a squeaky wheel.

The reality of these situations is that doctors sometimes sign imperfect contracts, and this can have repercussions on their career. There is a cultural problem in medicine where physicians have distanced themselves from the business and legal aspects of practicing medicine. Physicians need to empower themselves to understand the language in contracts and advocate for themselves in their contract negotiations.

Changes in Priorities Can Affect Leverage

A physician's ability to negotiate may change depending on the specialty, insurance coverage, and billing policies at any given time. If a given specialty is suddenly more productive for the group or hospital, the physician may be able to demand a higher salary or incentive pay.

The priorities of groups and health systems can also change year to year. This is especially true right now as many groups and health systems are consolidating into larger entities. An astute negotiator will have an understanding of the most current goals and financial needs of the organization.

What if my requests are denied?

By the time of the contract negotiation, the hiring parties have likely already invested time into a physician as a candidate. As long as the tone of the request is collegial, they will likely just say "no" if they cannot make the change or perhaps suggest some other modification. Even if they cannot accommodate a request, you may end up gaining more respect for standing up for yourself.

Most contracts I review require more than a few revisions before they are ready for signature. You never really know the motivations of the people hiring you, but you should not let that deter you from advocating for yourself. I have advised many physicians to walk away from contracts where they were getting a bad deal, and the hiring parties are not negotiating. It is a difficult thing to do at the time, but it can make a big difference in the career of a doctor. Most of the time, doctors that walk away from a bad deal end up in a better employment situation after assessing their options.

Talking about Money

If the money aspect of practicing medicine is something a physician does not feel comfortable talking about, they can look up data to bring to the table. Please refer back to the Fair Market Value and Compensation sections of this book for some information and cautions about different types of data available on physician compensation.

When negotiating salary, do the math and, if possible, humanize the request. Be realistic as to how much it will cost to live in a specific area, buy a house, and support a family. If a physician is relocating for a particular reason, they shouldn't be afraid to bring up why the move is significant if it may help their chances. It also helps to understand the feasibility of the practice or hospital paying a larger salary. Always factor in benefits to the total compensation package offered as it is the final cost of employment that matters to the employer.

Relationships, Trust, and Personalities

The question of trust comes up often. The culture in medicine is to trust superiors. When contracting for a position, a hiring doctor may be a superior, but they are not always the physician's advocate. Establish a good relationship with the hiring physician but do not trust them entirely, especially about issues that are not related to the practice of medicine. Even if a position is at a large institution that has heavily vetted contracts, some of the provisions may be drafted in favor of the institution to the physician's detriment.

For physicians just getting out of training, please remember that you are leaving a protected, academic, and almost "parental" environment for one of private contracting. It is important to understand that the hiring physicians have had no more formal training in contracts than physicians graduating today. They likely also do not know the implications of specific contract provisions. Make sure you are your own advocate, and if you don't understand something, seek help from a professional. Know what you are signing before you are bound by a contract. The contract is not just paper, it has meaning, and you now have an asset to protect—your medical license.

Promises Not Memorialized in the Agreement

It is very common for a physician to sign a contract with a new practice or group and be told that they will get a significant raise, partnership status, research funding, administrative time, office space, etc., within a few years. Sometimes, these terms are written into the agreement, but often they are not. An employer may want to exclude the terms from a contract so that they have some leeway if the relationship doesn't work out or if unexpected changes occur in their finances or ability to deliver on such promises. Other times, physicians are deliberately overpromised and will never receive the promised benefits.

If the promises are not explicitly stated in the contract, a physician must be prepared for them not to come to fruition. If a physician signs a contract that lacks a stated promise, it is in their best interest to have a detailed conversation with the hiring parties about the benefits and when they can be expected. It is then a judgment call on the physician's part as to whether they are willing to take the word of the hiring parties about whatever benefits are promised.

Be cautious of groups who refer to "gentleman's agreements," whether written or verbal, as these often do not contain necessary terms, and sometimes even contain contradictory terms. Make no mistake; if you sign a contract and something goes awry, the group will hire a lawyer who will hold you to the signed contract, not the gentleman's agreement that you were told you had.

Negotiation Takeaways

- Remember how much time you have put into training for this career and how important your medical license is for your ability to have a long successful career.

- Don't underestimate your worth.

- Familiarize yourself with the job responsibilities, local market salaries, benefits, and schedules.
- Minimize negotiating time and promptly respond to any correspondence regarding your requests.
- Create a relationship based on respect with your future employer.
- Be bold in what you are asking for or need, but also try to steer clear of being aggressive.
- Even if you have heard that salary is not negotiable in a particular area, always stand up for yourself and make sure you are not underpaid.

PART THREE

7. Narrative of a Sample Hiring Process

This section is an example of a hiring process; not all steps may be present in any specific situation. This section aims to show the importance of being involved in the early stages of contract formation and why it is so important for a physician to thoroughly read and understand their contract. Please follow a fictional doctor, Dr. Ana Smith, through her hiring process.

Dr. Ana Smith has interviewed and received a callback. She begins to discuss the position with the hiring physician and Human Resources (HR) representative. During the discussions with the hiring physician, basic contract terms are discussed. Basic contract terms include things like salary, benefits, work hours, schedule, etc. During this conversation, Dr. Smith negotiates the basic terms important for her to accept the position.

After Dr. Smith and the hiring physician decide on these terms, the terms are sent to HR to draft a letter of understanding. A letter of understanding (LOU) is a roughly 2-page document that sometimes but not always precedes a contract. The document can be confusing because the words “non-binding” typically appear across the top of the first page. "Non-binding" means that either party can walk away from the deal. However, if Dr. Smith wants the position, she should take this step with some gravity. An LOU represents the first "meeting of the minds" between Dr. Smith and her future employer. If she signs this letter and then requests completely different terms, it may be difficult to negotiate the new terms. Circumstances change, but Dr. Smith should make sure she is happy with what is contained in the LOU when it comes to her for signature.

Now that the basic terms are memorialized in the LOU, the contract can be drafted for Dr. Smith. Ideally, a legal department or lawyer will draft the contract, but this is often put in the hands of HR, or another individual altogether. Physicians, such as Dr. Smith, should never assume the hiring parties have an attorney drafting a contract, even in large institutions. If they do have an attorney, it is important to note that their attorney is looking out for their interests not necessarily those of Dr. Smith. During contract drafting, the basic terms will be added to a document along with a lot of legal language. It is important for Dr. Smith never to assume legal language is boilerplate language that does not need to be read. Dr. Smith needs to look out for herself and her medical license by carefully reviewing her contract before signing.

The contract should be reviewed for accuracy as to the terms Dr. Smith and her employers have agreed upon and for legality, equity, and compliance with other areas discussed in this book. Often there are legal terms that need to be altered or sections that need to be restructured in a contract. She should not assume that because something was discussed, it will be accurately reflected in the final contract. Discrepancies in agreed upon terms are where some of the more difficult negotiations may need to happen. An attorney can help guide her through this process and hopefully come out with a better contract for all parties in the end. Often the employer is the primary drafter of the contract. If Dr. Smith requests edits that are agreed upon, the employer will have the contract modified and sent back for Dr. Smith's approval. Note: Some employers prefer to have the physician or the physician's counsel modify the contract and send it back to them for review.

If a final contract is sent for signature before she has had a chance to review the edits, Dr. Smith should carefully review the changes before signing. If the contract is sent from an HR department, the contract may also be sent to the hiring physician, but he/she may only glance over it. The hiring physician often does not read the rest of the contract and is not Dr. Smith's advocate for anything contained within the agreement. It is Dr. Smith's responsibility as a contracting party to make sure she understands what is in the contract and how the provisions affect her.

8. How to Read a Contract

Physician contracts must be read carefully cover to cover. Missing and inaccurate terms are unfortunately common in physician contracts. Doctors are surprised when they receive a contract that does not cover the basic agreed upon terms. This chapter contains a short exercise in reading one section of a contract. If this exercise is not helpful, feel free to jump to Part Four of the book. Below is a section from a fictional Employment Contract with ABC Hospital Medical Group.

> The questions below are based on the following clause:
>
> "Purpose and Term of the Agreement: This employment agreement is entered into by and between ABC Medical Group, a California Professional Corporation, and Joe Smith, M.D., a physician Licensed to practice medicine in California, and provides that Physician will deliver Emergency Medical Services as an Employee of ABC Medical Group in ABC Hospital Emergency Medicine Department.
>
> The initial term of this Agreement shall be for one (1) year and shall commence on the Effective Date, July 1, 2020, and renew automatically for successive one-year terms absent proper notice from either party of intent to terminate the agreement."

Who are the parties to the Agreement?

The parties to the agreement are Joe Smith, M.D., and ABC Medical Group.

Why is the contact with ABC Medical Group and not directly with the hospital?

As we discussed earlier in the book, some states have a corporate practice of medicine doctrine which prohibits a business or corporation, for example, this hospital, from practicing medicine or employing a physician to provide professional services. With some exceptions, in states with such a doctrine, hospitals must develop separate medical groups or foundations controlled by other physicians in order to hire doctors and control the medical staff of the hospital. In this example, ABC Medical Group has been created to hire physicians. In many other states, the hospital would be able to contract to employ the physician directly.

What type of contract is this?

This is an employment contract for Emergency Medicine Services. A contract should state the type of contract and what type of services the physician will provide under the agreement. If the beginning of a contract contains so much legalese that one cannot understand what is going on, seek clarification. There is no reason for a contract to be written in obscure language. If the parties hiring a physician cannot explain what the contract says, there is a problem.

Where will the services be performed?

The services will be performed at ABC Hospital Emergency Medicine Department. It is best for the location of services to be specific and not left open-ended. Examples of open-ended clauses include, "In Los Angeles County" or "at other locations as the employer may determine from time to time." If a county is a small area, naming a whole county may be appropriate in some states. A contract should state all locations the physician is expected to work, with addresses if possible. If the location of services is too broad, the employer will have the ability to demand that the physician work at any location of their choosing within the parameters of the contract. This could lead to long commute times among other inconveniences. A better way to leave open the possibility of working at other locations is to state that the physician will work at other locations as mutually agreed. If there are multiple drafts of a contract floating around, be sure the final version has all of the correct terms. It is not unusual to see terms from an old draft show up in a final contract. Usually, this is due to a careless error rather than malicious intent.

When is the start date and how long is the term?

The start date of this contract is July 1, 2020, and the term is for one year. This contract has an automatic renewal provision, which means it will continue to renew for successive 1-year periods. When an agreement continues to roll over for consecutive terms like this, the signed agreement can sometimes be very different from the duties performed by the physician. If a physician signs a contract like this, they should always make sure the contract remains an accurate reflection of responsibilities and compensation. Some contracts terminate at the end of the contract; others renew with notice or automatically.

What are the services to be performed under the contract?

The services to be performed under this agreement are "Emergency Medicine Services." The services should be set out with sufficient specificity. This does not mean your contract must state you will see "X" number of patients over "Y" number of hours, although it can. The contract can state the type of medicine the physician is practicing, any agreed upon constraints, number of new patients, on-call schedule, administrative time, supervisory duties, etc.

9. Sample Contract

All contracts are written with different terms, order, and format. Most physician contracts are between 10-25 pages long, though some range up to about 50 pages when more complex arrangements are involved. The sample contract below consists of abbreviated, modified, and condensed commons clauses for educational purposes. The terms used in this sample contract may or may not appear in a contract and may have different headings or even no heading at all.

ABC HOSPITAL EMERGENCY DEPARTMENT PHYSICIAN EMPLOYMENT AGREEMENT

Purpose of Agreement: This employment agreement is entered into by and between ABC Medical Group, a California Professional Corporation, and Joe Smith, M.D., a Physician Licensed to practice medicine in California, and provides that Physician will deliver Emergency Medical Services as an Employee of ABC Medical Group in ABC Hospital Emergency Medicine Department.

Relationship of Parties and Duties of Physician: ABC Medical Group employs Physician to provide professional medical services on a full-time basis, in the specialty of Emergency Medicine.

Term of Employment: The initial term of this Agreement shall be for one (1) year and shall commence on the Effective Date, July 1, 2020, and renew automatically for successive one-year terms absent proper notice from either party of intent to terminate the agreement.

Billing of Claims and Reassignment of Professional Fees: Physician hereby assigns to Medical Group all professional fees earned for providing Emergency Medicine Services provided pursuant to this agreement. Physician shall look only to medical group for payment for services provided pursuant to this Agreement. Physician shall not under any circumstances seek compensation from, have any recourse against, or impose any additional charge to any patient.

Compensation and Benefits: Under this Agreement, Physician shall receive the compensation and employment benefits as outlined in this Agreement and incorporated by reference herein.

Professional Liability Insurance: ABC Medical Group agrees to provide professional liability insurance covering physician with a policy limit of at least $1 million per claim and with an aggregate claim limit of at least $3 million per year. In the event that the coverage is "claims made," ABC Medical Group will be solely responsible for assuming the cost of "tail" coverage.

Restrictive Covenants: Non-Competes, Confidentiality, and Non-Solicitation:
Non-Competition: During the term of this Agreement, Physician shall practice medicine exclusively for Employer and shall not without written consent of Employer, engage in any activity which constitutes the practice of medicine other than for Employer.

Confidentiality: Physician understands and acknowledges that Physician will have access to confidential information in the scope of employment. Physician agrees to keep all such information confidential and not use or disclose to others, any secrets or confidential technology, proprietary information, patient lists, or trade secrets of ABC Hospital or ABC Medical Group, without express written permission or as is required by the law.

Non-Solicitation: Physician agrees not to solicit business from patients, staff, or vendors for at least twelve months after this contract has terminated. Physician will have the right to inform patients that he/she is leaving the group by mail at physician's own expense.

Termination: This contract can be terminated by a) termination for cause, b) termination without cause, or c) termination with opportunity to cure a breach of contract.
Intellectual property: Any intellectual property, ownership rights, and profit generated from intellectual property of any kind created by Physician with use of Medical Group or Hospitals property or during the work hours of Physician, including but not limited to inventions, patents, copyrights, and software, shall be considered the intellectual property of the Employer.

Integration clause: This Agreement contains the complete expression of the rights and obligations of the Parties and shall supersede all other agreements, oral and written, which were previously made by the parties. This Agreement shall not be modified, amended, or supplemented, except in a written instrument executed by both Parties.

Arbitration: Parties agree to use good faith negotiations to resolve any dispute, claim, or controversy that may arise under this agreement. In the event that the parties are unable to resolve any dispute, it will be settled in arbitration.

Indemnification: Except as covered by insurance, Group shall indemnify and hold harmless Physician for all acts or omissions within the scope of employment. Where Physician is found to be grossly negligent or acting outside of the scope of employment, Physician agrees to indemnify and hold harmless Group for all damages and fees related to Physician's grossly negligent acts or omissions.

Signatures: All parties to be bound should sign the contract.

PART FOUR

Key Concepts:

- "Term of Years" vs. "Terms" of a Contract
- Contract Renewal
- Termination
- Death or Disability of Physician
- Breach of Contract
- Possible Consequences of Breaking a Contract

10. Term and Termination

The term of an agreement is the length in months or years. The usage of the word "term" or "term of years" in the singular refers to the length of the agreement. When discussing a contract, "terms" or "terms of the contract" in the plural is used to discuss the different areas of the contract such as compensation, hours, locations, etc.

Sample Contract Language:

"This contract shall commence on January 1, 2020, and shall continue for one (1) year, subject to the termination provisions of this agreement. This agreement may be extended or renewed by mutual agreement of the contracting parties."

In the sample language above, the contract is for a one-year term and may renew upon mutual agreement of the parties. A few months before the contract expires, the physician should be presented with a new agreement or begin to negotiate the terms of a new contract. This is a good time for a physician to re-evaluate all areas of the contract with a year or more of experience under their belt. If the physician is not presented with an updated contract, the physician should initiate the conversation, as it is important to have a current contract that accurately expresses responsibilities and compensation.

Contract Term and Renewal

Contracts vary in length and renewal term. A contract may state it is a one-year agreement with automatic renewal, meaning that it will automatically renew for another one-year term. Sometimes there is language present stating that in order to prevent automatic renewal, notice must be given for example 30, 60, or 90 days before the expiration of the initial term. This section of the contract should be read very carefully to make sure the term and renewal language are clear. A physician should consent to the term and be sure they can comply with all notice requirements. A five-year contract may require as much as six months or a full year notice to express intent to terminate the agreement.

Contract Term vs. "At Will"

If a contract is for a term of years, for example, three years, it should be clearly stated in the agreement. Contracts that do not have a defined end date are referred to as “at-will” contracts. “At-will" means the contract can be terminated by either the physician or employer at any time without a supporting reason or cause.[36] As a simple example, a job in a clothing store or retail outlet is almost always “at-will.” In the retail setting, it is customary but not required to give two weeks’ notice before leaving. Under an “at will” physician employment agreement, it is customary to provide notice and the patient abandonment laws of the state must be taken into consideration. However, technically the doctor can walk off the job at any time and be fired at any time.

It is important to note that “at-will” does not mean “at random” in most states. The California Supreme Court has made it clear that employers have the right to terminate employees without cause, provided the employees have been put on notice at the time of hiring that they are “at will.”[37] However, other judicial decisions make it clear that employees may not be terminated in a manner that is discriminatory or when doing so is against public policy. Essentially, while one may be terminated for no reason or an arbitrary reason, one cannot be terminated for an unlawful reason.[38] This is something to keep in mind in the event a physician is fired for what they believe to be an unlawful reason.

Contract Termination

Termination is another way of saying the contract has ended either voluntarily or involuntarily. If a physician is bound to a contract for a term of years, it is very important to review how the contract can terminate before the end of the agreement. Valid termination provisions include "for cause" termination, "not for cause" termination, termination by law, or on the occurrence of an event. If there are no defined parameters in a contract for termination, then a physician may have to breach the contract to exit before the end of the term. A contract can sometimes terminate on mutual agreement. If the parties do not agree, and the contract is not performed by one party, the other party may sue for breach of contract and the parties will end up in litigation or arbitration.

Termination "For Cause"

Termination "for cause" in the simplest terms means that one party has done something wrong or broken one of the terms of the contract and the other party is terminating because of the breach. Depending on the contract, termination may be immediate or occur after notice has been provided.[39] Physicians should use caution to ensure the employer does not give themselves too much leeway under this section. For example, the employer should not be able to terminate a physician for any reason they want. The "for cause" termination provisions should be specific and limited to reasons that would directly undermine the intent of the contract or potentially harm patients.

It is common for a contract to contain a long list of detailed, legitimate reasons the contract can be immediately terminated and then have the last one say something to the effect of, "for any reason employer deems appropriate." This is too broad and should not be included in a contract. There can be consequences to having a contract terminated "for cause." One such consequence is being reported to the medical board, so physicians must be careful about signing a contract with provisions that are too broadly worded in this section.

> Sample Contract Language:
>
> "Employer shall have the right to terminate this Agreement for cause effective immediately with the delivery of notice to Employee upon the occurrence of any of the following events: if Employee ceases to be a licensed physician; Employee's DEA license is revoked; if Employer and Employee mutually agree in writing to termination; if Employee becomes permanently disabled or incapacitated, as determined in accordance with this Agreement; if Employee is convicted of a felony under any state or federal law."

Some contracts contain stipulations for terminating the contract for "good cause" where an employer would have a heightened burden of establishing the reasons why a particular employee is terminated.

Some valid reasons to immediately terminate a contract include:

- License suspension or revocation
- Medical board action against the physician
- Illegal drug use
- Inability to perform essential functions of the job
- Felony conviction
- Suspension or exclusion from insurance plans or payors
- Inability to renew DEA license

Termination "Without Cause" by Employer or Physician

"Without cause" termination means that a contract can be terminated with no stated reason as long as proper notice is provided as prescribed by the contract. Not all contracts contain a voluntary termination provision. A physician and employer can contract for this type of provision, where appropriate, as a way to end the contract before the end of the term. A contract may state a number of days or months' notice needed for termination under such a provision. A contract that automatically renews may have a termination provision stating the physician must give notice a certain number of days before the renewal date to prevent the automatic renewal of the contract.

> Sample Contract Language:
>
> "This employment agreement can be terminated on the election of either the employer or physician upon 60 days' written notice."

Though there are many benefits to a notice period for termination, there can also be downsides. Life can be unpredictable, and for some positions and some practitioners, it is nice to have this flexibility. On the other hand, contracts can provide stability. If either side can voluntarily terminate the contract with a short amount of notice, it erodes some of the stability and security of a contract. Employers sometimes try to change some terms of the contract, including compensation, knowing that if the physician does not agree, they can give notice to the physician and replace them within a short amount of time.

Termination by Employer with Opportunity to Cure

A beneficial addition to a contract is to allow an opportunity to "cure" or fix a technical breach of contract. A cure period is a time frame under which there is a technical default of the contract, but the contract is not considered to be in default if the problem can be remedied within the stated time.[40]

> Sample Contract Language:
>
> "Employer may terminate this agreement, following written notice and Physician's failure to cure such breach within 30 days, in the event that the Physician breaks any provision of this agreement or is deficient in his/her performance under this agreement. If Physician fails to cure such breach within this time, Employer has the right to terminate immediately."

Often this will fall under the termination "for cause" section of an agreement and only applies to certain provisions. For example, the failure to timely renew a medical license is a technical breach of most medical contracts. Without a license, the physician is temporarily unable to work, but the contract may provide an amount of time, generally from thirty to sixty days to cure the breach of contract and allow the physician to come back to work. This is a provision that is nice to have as sometimes there are administrative hold-ups or human errors.

Termination on Death or Disability

A contract may state that it will terminate on the death or permanent disability of the physician as shown below in the sample contract language. The time period stated in the contract determines if the disability is permanent or significant enough under the terms of the contract to justify the termination of the agreement.

> Sample Contract Language:
>
> "Employer shall have the right to terminate this Agreement effective immediately if Employee suffers a disability that renders Employee unable to perform his duties under this agreement for a period of 180 days within a 365-day period or upon the death of the Employee."

The sample language above denotes that the Employee must be unable to perform his work duties for at least half of the year to cancel the agreement for permanent disability. Sixty days within a six-month period or ninety days with a one-year period are also common. I have reviewed contracts with a threshold as low as fifteen days in a six-month period. If this type of short disability period arises in a contract, one should consider asking for revisions to the contract. A surgery or bad flu can keep a physician out of work for a few weeks. A common ailment that will improve in a reasonable amount of time should not be grounds to terminate a contract for disability.

Termination within a Probationary Period

Some contracts establish a probationary period when a physician begins providing medical services to patients. A probationary period in a physician contract is a trial period to make sure the physician is a good fit for the organization and vice versa. The parameters depend on the specifics of the agreement, but if there is a probationary period, generally during this three to six-month time, a physician is free to leave their employment and employer is free to fire the physician without any contractual repercussions.

> Sample Contract Language:
>
> "The first six months of this Agreement will comprise of a probationary period. During this period, Employee's performance will be periodically evaluated by Employer and Employee will be mentored by senior Physicians where appropriate. At the end of the probationary period, a final review will be conducted by Employer. If after the final review, either Employer or Employee decide this position is not a good fit for Employee, this contract will terminate immediately without cause or penalty to either party."

Carefully read the parameters of any specific probationary period and seek out counsel where there are concerns. Government and nonprofit employers are more likely to have such clauses in their contract because in such institutions policies may make it difficult to fire an employee after formal hiring. Building a trial period into the contract allows for much more flexibility if the parties decide the job is not a good fit for the individual.

Termination by Law, "Act of God," or Occurrence of An Event

Another clause that often shows up in a contract is one that states the contract can be terminated if there is a change in the law, or an "Act of God" makes the contract impossible to continue. For "Termination by Law" think of a change in regulations that forces a group or clinic to shut down. For "Act of God" think something along the lines of a hospital being destroyed by fire or an earthquake.

In addition to these reasons, a contract may be conditioned on the maintenance of certain hospital or insurance contracts. This means that if an event, such as the termination of the specific contract occurs, it could terminate the employment agreement. It is very important to understand all of the ways a contract can terminate, even if some seem unlikely at the time of signing.

Breach of Contract, Liquidated Damages, and Injunctive Relief

A breach of contract is a failure to live up to the terms of the contract or taking affirmative actions against the obligations or terms of the agreement.[41] Liquidated damages provisions are used as a means to compensate the employer for the breach of an employment contract where damages might otherwise be difficult to ascertain with certainty.[42]

> Sample Contract Language:
>
> "The parties acknowledge that it may be impractical or impossible to determine the actual damages the Group will suffer if Physician breaches his/her obligations under this agreement and the Group is unable to retain a suitable replacement practitioner quickly. Therefore, all parties agree, if Physician breaches the agreement, Physician will immediately pay Group the sum of $25,000 as liquidated damages, not as a penalty. The parties agree the sum represents a fair and reasonable estimate of damages that Group will suffer as a result of the loss of a medical practitioner prior to the expiration of the term of the agreement."

Liquidated Damages clauses are often present in physician contracts and act as a deterrent to a sudden termination of a contract. An example of a sudden contract termination might be an ER doctor walking off the job in the middle of a particularly stressful shift. In many states these clauses are based on estimates of lost-profits, damages, or out of pocket expenses an employer estimates they will incur if they suddenly lose a physician that staffs a clinic or a hospital. The law generally assumes that the right sum of money can fix all problems, so these clauses may contain a fixed amount of money a physician will owe if they suddenly walk off the job or breach the contract. In my experience, in California, the dollar amount typically ranges anywhere from $5,000 to $80,000 for physician employment contracts.

The same clause or another area of the contract may also provide for "injunctive relief." "Injunctive relief" means that money will not be an adequate solution and allows the employer to ask a court to stop the physician from doing whatever they are doing that violates the contract and is causing harm.[43] This becomes particularly important if the physician is violating the contract by sharing confidential information or competing with a former employer in violation of a valid non-competition agreement. If the physician only has to pay damages and not stop whatever they are doing, it could irreparably hurt the former employer.

Courts do allow and uphold these types of liquidated damages and injunctive relief clauses where they are reasonable and do not appear to be a punishment. If the fixed amount of liquidated damages is high, it can often be negotiated down in the contract. Small groups and practices will often overestimate as a form of deterrence and to make sure they are covered in the event of a breach of contract by a physician. A physician has the right to question the number placed in the contract and try to determine if it is a somewhat accurate representation of harm in the event of a breach. There certainly are situations where the liquated damages are set arbitrarily and are unreasonably high.

Forfeiture of Bonuses or Incentive Pay for Early Termination

According to California law and the laws of many states, most earned benefits such as wages and vacation time cannot be forfeited involuntarily.[44] This means in a state with such a law; one cannot be forced to give up pay for work they have already completed or benefits that have been earned if the contract terminates before the end of the term. Retention bonuses and funds promised if one remains employed can be forfeited for early termination in many states. If there are any loan terms in the contract, either an income guarantee or housing loan forgiveness program, a physician can be forced to pay back the outstanding balance of the loan upon early termination of the agreement if the repayment and forfeiture terms are clearly defined in the contract.

Waiver of Due Process Rights on Termination

There will be a whole chapter dedicated to the due process rights a physician has in their privileges and licensing as a physician. As you read, please remember that a clause asking a physician to waive their right to a hearing before termination can sometimes show up in the termination section. A physician should very carefully consider whether it is worth it to them or not to sign such a waiver. Please see Chapter 18 for more information about "Hospital Privileges and Due Process."

Common Questions

Is it better to have an "at-will" contract or a five-year contract?

This question will have a different answer for every physician as it is a very personal choice. Some physicians enjoy the mobility and freedom of a short or at-will contract, while others enjoy the security of a long-term agreement. There are too many factors to be considered to provide a universal answer to this question.

If "without cause" or "not for cause" termination provisions are not present in my contract, should I request they be added?

Similar to the question above, this can be a personal decision. Without-cause termination provisions provide some flexibility. I believe they are a good option, especially for younger physicians who tend to change jobs more frequently than mid-level or late career physicians. However, if the physician has the right to terminate without cause, most likely so does the employer so there is no guarantee of continued employment. This is something everyone needs to decide based on his or her circumstances and career goals.

What do I do if I think I am wrongfully terminated?

Seek the assistance from an employment lawyer to discuss the merits of the case as soon as possible.

My employer is trying to change the terms of the contract after it has been signed. What can I do?

Contracts are binding, so you can attempt to hold your employer to the contract. Unfortunately, many times when this happens, there is also a short without cause termination provision. This may mean that the employer can decide to terminate the physician's contract within 30 or 60 days at which time the physician would be out of a job. It is best to seek advice from an attorney as to your specific situation. Each one of these cases is unique, but it can certainly put a physician in a difficult position when the employer wants to change a term, especially if that term is the compensation, work hours, or location of work.

Key Concepts:

- Professional Liability Insurance
- Types of Malpractice Coverage and Limits
- Responsibility for Paying for Coverage
- Tail and Nose Coverage
- Other Types of Insurance

11. Professional Liability and Insurance

Insurance is an important consideration for physicians in any type of medical practice. A physician in private practice may need to consider a few more types of insurance than one working for a large health system, but the same overall coverage needs apply. This chapter will look at different types of insurance and provide examples of how this coverage should be explained in a contract.

Professional Liability Insurance

Professional liability or "malpractice" insurance protects a physician and the employer from claims related to the negligent practice of medicine.[45] Two common types of professional liability coverage carried by major insurance companies are "claims-made" and "occurrence" policies.[46] Some large groups and hospitals have their own insurance trust, explained below, instead of using a major carrier for professional liability insurance. Each trust and policy functions in a slightly different manner and may or may not cover the tail insurance for all physicians in the hospital system or group.

Sample Contract Language:

> "ABC Medical Group will provide professional liability insurance for Physician with a policy limit of at least $1 million per claim and with an aggregate claim limit of at least $3 million per year. In the event the physician is no longer employed by Medical Group, Physician will be responsible for obtaining tail insurance."

Limits and coverage can vary significantly between specialties, but the majority of physicians will carry a policy with a $1 million per incident and $3 million in the aggregate annual limit. Limits apply regardless of the type of policy, and a physician who is sued will be covered for a specific incident subject to the terms of the policy.

Claims-Made Policy vs. Occurrence Policy

A claims-made policy covers a physician for the period of time premiums are paid. If premiums are only paid for the 2019 calendar year and a claim is brought in 2020 for an incident that occurred in 2019, the physician must have "tail insurance" in order for the claim to be covered. Tail coverage will be discussed in detail below.

An occurrence policy covers a physician for any claims during the period of time the physician is insured under the plan. If a physician has coverage and pays the premium for only the year 2019, and there is ever a claim filed against that physician for something that took place in 2019, it should be covered. Tail coverage or extended reporting coverage is generally not required with occurrence coverage, with the caveat that individual policies do vary.

Insurance Trust or Self-Insurance Policy

A private insurance trust or self-insurance policy can function as either a "claims-made" or "occurrence" policy. Large institutions often have enough employees to establish a risk pool of their own in the form of an insurance trust. Instead of contracting with a third-party insurance company, the institution or physicians pay into a trust that maintains funds to cover litigation costs and judgments/settlements for malpractice claims. These arrangements are generally safe and as good as a third-party insurer, but they should be looked at with a little more scrutiny depending on the size of the organization. Sometimes these policies have more restrictions on the physician and the type of claims that are covered. They also may give the employer or holder of the trust policy the right to settle claims and manage the direction of the case. This may mean a physician is forced to settle a claim that they might otherwise wish to fight in court or arbitration.

Tail Coverage (Extended Reporting Endorsement)

Tail coverage, also called Extended Reporting Endorsement, is necessary when a physician leaves a position with a "claims-made" policy in place. Tail coverage covers claims originating from the time period under which the physician was covered by the policy but filed after they are no longer on the policy. There are a few different options for tail coverage. The first is stand-alone tail coverage, which is usually paid for in a lump sum payment often ranging from 150% to 250% of the annual malpractice coverage premiums. Depending on the specialty this lump sum payment can range from about $30,000 to well over $100,000 or more. The inclusion of full tail insurance in a policy is not something to be taken lightly. It is a big benefit.

> Sample Contract Language with tail insurance:
>
> "ABC Medical Group agrees to provide professional liability insurance covering physician with a policy limit of at least $1 million per claim and with an aggregate claim limit of at least $3 million per year. In the event that the coverage is 'claims made,' ABC Medical Group will be solely responsible for assuming the cost of 'tail' coverage."

The second option when purchasing tail coverage is to pay a lower fee to be covered for a defined number of years, as opposed to for any claims filed in the future. The number of years is usually determined by the specific state's statute of limitation for medical claims. This can be a good option but depends on the specialty. It is considered the safest route to have tail coverage that will cover a physician indefinitely.

A third option is for a group or hospital to keep the physician on the malpractice indefinitely as a way of providing coverage for acts after the physician has left the position. If the physician is never taken off a claims-made policy, then they will always be covered. The flaw in this option is that coverage can only be guaranteed while the group or hospital is on the same malpractice plan with the same carrier. If they change the coverage or lose such coverage, it could put all of their former employees or contracted physicians at risk. This option is often presented to a physician during the negotiation process as "full tail coverage." Use caution to distinguish this option from stand-alone full tail coverage.

Some organizations will cover tail coverage after a physician has been employed for a few years or start to cover a larger percentage of the coverage each year a physician works for the organization. For example, one can negotiate that after two years, 50% of the policy will be covered, and after five years, it will be covered 100%.

Nose Coverage (Continuous Coverage)

If a physician switches from one job to another or one group to another, they can often ask the new malpractice carrier to provide continuous coverage with so-called "nose coverage." Instead of purchasing tail insurance through the prior employer, coverage for prior acts is purchased through the new employer's policy. It depends on the insurer and the claims history of the physician, but this type of coverage is generally cheaper than stand-alone tail coverage. It is important to check if an employment contract will allow a physician to obtain nose coverage (continuous coverage) instead of requiring the purchase of a stand-alone policy.

> Sample Contract Language:
>
> "Tail insurance will be the sole responsibility of the Employee. Employee may choose to purchase a new malpractice policy or obtain a policy through a new group that will provide continuous coverage for prior acts from the time Employee first received coverage under Employer's malpractice plan."

Occasionally, employers require a physician to purchase complete coverage after a contract ends and specify this in the contract. It provides more protection for the employer to have a physician covered for all prior acts. If a physician purchases coverage with a new employer and ends up leaving that position, the former employer may not have a guarantee that they remain covered. However, it is always in the physician's best interest to remain covered, and a physician can save quite a bit of money by utilizing this continuous coverage option where possible.

Common Questions about Professional Liability Insurance

How do I know what type of coverage I have?

Ask. The only way to know what kind of coverage you are being provided with is to ask the employer. If it is a smaller group or practice, it is a good idea to ask for a copy of the policy to review. Many employers are hesitant to provide the full policy but should be able to provide a certificate of insurance that states the policy limits and exclusions. If a policy is specifically procured for an individual physician, then that individual's name should be listed on the certificate of insurance.

Who is responsible for paying the premium?

As an employee, generally but not always the premium for malpractice coverage will be covered by the employer as a benefit of employment. As an independent contractor, a physician is often asked to pay the premium on his or her plan or secure their own malpractice insurance. Even for an independent contractor, many hiring entities are willing to cover the cost of the coverage. In some specialties and some states, where doctors are often hired as contractors when they should be employees, the policy really should be covered by the group or hospital due to the nature of the work.

How important is tail insurance and do I need it for part-time positions?

Tail insurance is very important for physicians at all stages of their careers. It is never advisable for a physician to leave themselves open to liability, whether it is for a full-time job or a moonlighting gig once a month.

Professional Liability and Indemnification

A clause such as the one below will typically show up in an employment agreement. In many states, including California, an employer must indemnify and hold a physician harmless for things that happen under the scope of their employment.[47] This clause is often subject to insurance requirements and may not cover an employee if their acts are found to be outside of the scope of employment.[48]

> Sample Contract Language:
>
> "Employer agrees to indemnify and hold physician harmless for any acts or decisions made in good faith while performing services for Employer. Employer will pay for all expenses, including reasonable attorney fees, actually or necessarily incurred by physician in connection with the defense of any action that has been brought against Physician in connection with Physician's employment."

The clause may go on to state that the employer will take over the day to day litigation of a malpractice case and have the right to make settlement decisions on behalf of the physician. On the one hand, this can be good as most physicians do not want to get tied down with a lawyer and have to worry too much about the paperwork involved. On the other hand, the physician may be giving up some control over their reputation, since such a clause can allow a case to be settled or even admit fault in a case that the physician might have otherwise wanted to continue to fight. Each contract is unique and should be read and negotiated carefully. It is especially important to look at the interplay between this type of clause and other indemnification clauses which will be discussed in a later Chapter 16.

Errors & Omissions and Director & Officers Insurance

Errors and Omissions insurance (E&O) protects a physician against risks associated with non-patient care activities such as training, compliance, and oversight of employees. These are activities which may be part of a physician's job description, but not covered under a malpractice policy.

Director and Officers (D&O) insurance is important for legal claims involving internal mismanagement; and wrongful acts or omissions while in a director or officer capacity.

Both of these types of insurance are especially important if a physician is performing high-level administrative tasks in addition to their role as a medical care provider or a member of a board of directors.

Medical Directors

There is a whole chapter in the last section of the book discussing medical directorships. For this chapter, please note that many standard malpractice insurance policies have a Medical Director Exclusion. An exclusion means that the actions of a medical director may not be covered by the employer's plan. If this is the case, the plan will need a separate medical director rider attached. I always recommend that an individual Medical Director try to procure this rider with their name written and included in the policy.

Special Services

Some contracts and specialties have unique requirements which should be detailed in the contract. Take for example if a physician is an Emergency Room doctor who is asked to deal with in-house emergencies in other areas of the hospital outside of the ER. For a physician in a specialty that has such a unique requirement, there are a few questions to ask to clarify rights and responsibilities. Using this example of an ER doctor:

1. Does the physician have the right to refuse to provide care outside of the ER for ANY reason, or only if it will jeopardize the ER patients?
2. Does the malpractice policy cover the physician outside of the ER? If the malpractice is only for the ER, then

the physician should not be asked to cover anywhere else and would be putting themselves at risk to provide care elsewhere in the hospital.

3. Is the physician privileged elsewhere in the hospital or only in the ER? If not, then they should not be asked to cover other areas of the hospital.

Auto Insurance

Many contracts ask a physician to add their employer as a secondary insured on their personal automobile insurance. A contract may even demand a certain level of coverage for a personal automobile. This is to protect against lawsuits the employer may face if a physician is driving a personal car on business errands or coming to or from work and injures someone in an accident. The person injured may be able to attach your employer's name to a lawsuit. These clauses vary in demands and sometimes employers don't care that much about them. Many insurers will add an employer as a secondary insured at no extra charge. Physicians have had these clauses removed from contracts simply by asking. If an employer demands a level of insurance that is costly for the physician, it may be worth asking for a reimbursement for extra costs.

Life and Disability Insurance

Life and disability insurance may be important if a physician has a family or is in a specialty that demands them to work with their hands or remain physically active. It is best to speak to an advisor that specializes in this type of insurance to determine appropriate coverage levels. It is advisable to secure disability insurance early in your career, separate from any policies that may be offered by an employer. Employer-based policies often terminate with employment, and it may become more difficult to obtain disability insurance as physicians age.

Key Concepts:

- Non-Competition Agreements
- Exclusivity During Employment
- Moonlighting
- Post Termination Restrictions
- Non-Solicitation of Patients, Employees, and Vendors
- Confidentiality and Non-Disclosure Provisions

12. Restraints on Competition and Confidentiality

The majority of a contract lays out the affirmative responsibilities of each party under the agreement. Restrictive covenants and restrictions on competition place restraints by contract on what a doctor can do at work; in their own time; and after the contract has terminated. A few of the most common forms of restrictive covenants in physician contracts include exclusivity during employment; post-employment restrictions; non-solicitation agreements; and confidentiality agreements. These restrictive covenants are important to read thoroughly and have reviewed by an attorney. The information and rules in this chapter vary significantly from state to state. California law is heavily referenced in this section by way of example. Please be sure to research the laws in the appropriate state or seek the help of an advisor in the applicable jurisdiction.

California is one of a handful of states that with few exceptions, outright rejects certain restrictive covenants because the state has established strong public policy in favor of allowing open competition and free movement of employees between employers.[49] Other states use a "rule of reasonableness" when determining if a restriction on competition and free movement is valid. Under the rule of reasonableness, courts look at whether or not the restriction is reasonable in scope and duration.[50] California has expressly rejected the "rule of reasonableness," and the state continues to favor open competition in both statutory authority and case law.[51]

Covenants Not-to-Compete

A covenant-not-to-compete, or non-competition agreement, is a clause or attachment to a contract that restricts the signer's ability to freely practice their profession or compete with an employer while employed or after employment has terminated. The next few sections will explain the differences between covenants not-to-compete during employment and post-termination.

Exclusivity. During Employment Non-Compete

"Exclusivity" is a legal term which, in most physician employment contracts, means the physician will not be permitted to provide professional medical services for any other institution or any patients other than those of the employer while the physician is employed.[52]

> Sample Contract Language:
>
> "During the term of this Agreement, Physician shall not without the written consent of Employer engage in any activity which constitutes or relates to the practice of medicine other than for or on behalf of Employer."

In most states, employers can restrict a physician's ability to provide patient care outside of their group or organization while employed with them. This restriction can only apply for a true employment arrangement and should be limited to employees who are contracted full time.[53] Exclusivity is based on a common law duty of loyalty owed to an employer.[54] This has been codified into the laws of most states. The idea is that all employees owe their employer a duty to act in the employer's best interest and therefore not compete with the employer. An exclusivity clause can have an exception stating that a physician may ask the employer for written permission to perform work outside of their duties under the contract. The sample clause above is an example, but be aware the wording of these clauses can vary quite a bit, so it is important to read each contract carefully.

Moonlighting, Passion Projects, and other Employment While Employed

If an exclusivity clause is present in a contract, and the physician has a moonlighting position or would like to pursue other interests outside of full-time employment, I recommend talking to the hiring parties. In some specialties, it is common for doctors to have multiple jobs. The new employer may not have an issue with the other position or project, but it is in everyone's best interest for it to be out in the open. The last thing anyone wants is to assume that it will be fine to continue a research project, work on outside inventions, or moonlight somewhere else and then find out that the employer does not consent to such outside activities under the contract. If it is unclear whether a project or a position falls within an exclusivity clause, consult with an attorney or discuss it with the hiring parties if appropriate.

Independent Contractors

As an independent contractor, a physician should not be asked to sign an exclusivity clause. The whole point of being an independent contractor, both for legal determinations and practical reasons, is to allow for non-exclusive work. Independent contractors do not owe the same duty of loyalty that employees do to their employers and their right to work cannot be restrained.[55] If such a clause arises in an independent contractor agreement, the physician should consult an attorney and request removal. Independent contractor agreements may ask a contractor to sign a clause that states they will not do any work that would materially impact their ability to perform the essential functions of their job under the agreement. This language is generally considered acceptable.

Post Termination Restrictions

A post-termination non-compete clause is one that prohibits a physician from competing with a former employer after employment has ended for a limited time and in a limited geographic area.[56] In many states, this type of clause is valid and quite restrictive.

> Sample Contract Language:
>
> "Physician shall not, during the term of this agreement or for a period of three (3) years from the date this agreement is terminated, provide professional medical services, directly or indirectly in competition with Employer within thirty (30) mile radius from any of Employer's offices."

These clauses can be very challenging to negotiate and can create a lot of hardship when a physician leaves a position and has to obtain a new job outside of the restricted area. If a physician is unable to work within 30 miles of their current job, it may mean a significant commute time or worse having to move themselves or their family to find a new job for the next three years. If there are children and a spouse involved, they may be uprooted as well and have to find new work and schools. A physician should carefully consider the ramifications of such a clause, especially if the physician practices a specialty that carries its own inherent restrictions on location or equipment needs.

There are many ways to modify these provisions, one such way is to look at how reasonable and necessary the "restricted area" is to accomplish the employer's goal of not having competition. In a city, a few miles might be enough not to feel competition, whereas in a rural area or a more specialized field a whole county might be reasonable. Also, consider if the restricted area is based on a radius from the primary location of the employer or if it is based on a number of miles from any office or hospital location the employer has any business. If it is the latter, there should be a thorough discussion as to what is really necessary and fair for the employee. Ultimately, where these clauses are valid, the physician has to balance how much the restriction could potentially cause problems and stress with the compensation and opportunity the position presents.

Some states, including California, consistently find covenants not-to-compete with a former employer or contracts with penalties for such competition, to be void and unenforceable on public policy grounds.[57] The terms "void" and "unenforceable" mean that they will not likely be enforced by the courts. Even though they are unenforceable in most cases, post-termination non-compete clauses do show up in contracts in California. If such a clause is present in a contract in a state that favors open competition, the physician should not sign the contract with the clause intact unless an exception applies. Leaving such a clause in the contract can leave the physician open to unnecessary dispute, and there are unfortunately times when such clauses are wrongfully upheld.

Post termination covenants-not-to-compete in California are only enforceable for physicians in narrow cases where there is a sale of a practice or all assets of the practice; or the dissolution of a significant ownership share or partnership agreement.[58] If a contract might fall into one of these categories, it would be best to consult an attorney to determine if the non-compete is valid before signing. Some states also have restrictions on the number of miles and years that are reasonable in a post-termination non-competition agreement. In California, the policy of open competition is enforced equally for independent contractors and employees.[59]

Non-Solicitation Clauses

It is common for physician contracts to contain provisions that limit solicitation of either employees, vendors, or patients of a practice after employment has terminated. These clauses are a type of non-compete, but even in restrictive states, courts have been more lenient on allowing the clauses to stand if they are protecting an employer's legitimate trade secrets.[60]

Sample Contract Language:

> "Physician shall have the right to inform patients that he/she is leaving the group, but shall not directly or indirectly solicit patients, staff, or vendors for business for at least 12 months after contract termination."

Employee non-solicitation clauses and slightly more restrictive non-interference clauses are a way for an employer to limit a former employee from competing by "raiding" the staff or clientele of the former employer. California law technically has a firm stance that one employee may solicit another to leave current employment and associate with a competing business if the solicited employee is not under a contract of employment.[61] However, practically speaking, if contractual provisions limiting solicitation are found to be reasonable in scope and tied to a need to protect trade secrets, they are often allowed by courts.[62] The justifications for these clauses vary state to state, but courts have recognized that employers put a lot of time into building a patient base and recruiting and training staff, so these restraints are used to protect those investments. Such a clause generally needs to contain a limit on the term of the non-solicitation provisions and be reasonable in scope.[63] Again, what is typical or allowed varies quite a bit state to state.

Patient Solicitation

Some contracts state that the physician cannot contact or solicit patients of the practice or hospital after they are no longer employed by or affiliated with the practice or hospital. This is another area that varies significantly from state to state. In open competition states, such as California, assuming there is not a valid post-employment non-compete, a former employee is free to solicit business from former employer's customers if the competition is "fairly and legally conducted."[64] When a patient non-solicitation provision is valid, it should only apply to current patients of the practice, not to patients that have come to the practice since the relevant contract has terminated. Patients generally have the option of following their doctor even if the physician is barred from soliciting patients for a certain amount of time. Every state's rules and restrictions are a bit different in this regard so be sure to research or consult with someone knowledgeable about the law in the applicable state.

For physicians, this means that if such a clause is present in a contract, even if it is limited in scope and duration, the validity of such a clause may depend on the circumstances. If any of the wording of the clause is too broad or limits competition in a way that is too restrictive, it may require some negotiation before signing.

Prohibition Against Patient Abandonment

Contracts often contain a clause prohibiting a physician from abandoning patients or terminating care before the patient has been transferred to another physician.[65] California prohibitions against patient abandonment require a physician to either see through the care of a patient or ensure they are transferred to another physician who can continue their care.[66] In many situations, for both small group and large hospitals, a physician will find a clause in their contract that says they must remain on staff even after termination if their patients still need care. This is a common clause and generally valid.

Confidentiality Agreements and Non-Disclosure Agreements (NDA)

Confidentiality Agreements and Non-Disclosure Agreements are agreements included in a contract or as an addendum to a contract used to protect a business' proprietary information, trade secrets, and confidential information. These agreements are valid and enforceable as long as they are not written too broadly and are drafted in such a way that it is clear what information is protected under the agreement.[67]

> Sample Contract Language:
>
> "Physician understands and acknowledges that Physician will have access to confidential information in the scope of employment. Physician agrees to keep all such information confidential and not use or disclose to others, any secrets or confidential technology, proprietary information, patient lists, or trade secrets of ABC

Hospital or ABC Medical Group, without express, written permission or as is required by the law."

Most contracts place some restrictions on what information a physician can share outside of the organization both while employed and for a time after employment. The section often states that the physician has access to some of the corporation's confidential information from time to time and that they should not disclose it to others. Businesses and individuals have the right to protect their confidential information and trade secrets. To be classified as a trade secret, the material or information must actually be confidential and fall under the definition of a trade secret. Patient lists and research data generated in practices have been found to be trade secrets.[68] The employer's determination of what is a trade secret is not dispositive. To be considered confidential, information must be treated as confidential information. It must be clear to the physician what is and what is not protected, for example, by writing the word "confidential" on all pertinent documents.[69] Ultimately it would be up to a judge to determine if the information is truly confidential or a trade secret.

Common Questions

In states where non-competes are not enforceable, why might an employer or contractor try to put one of these clauses into a contract?

I always like to give the benefit of the doubt; there is always a chance that the contract was adapted from a contract in another state and the provision is a holdover that has not been removed. The first step to negotiating the removal of such a provision where it may not be valid is to explain that the clause is not enforceable and simply request that the clause is removed. If that doesn't work, one may have to start thinking of other reasons for the inclusion of a provision that is unenforceable.

Groups and hospitals sometimes knowingly include such provisions to deter a physician from competing or to strong-arm a physician into complying with a provision, even though it is not legal in the state. Physicians may feel they need to comply with a clause that is in a contract they signed even if they know it may not be enforceable simply because they agreed to it by contract. The employer knows a doctor would have to take them to court to challenge such a clause, and that is unlikely to happen. If they are taken to court, the employer would likely receive no more than a slap on the wrist from a court for including it. It should be noted at least in California; if an employer refuses to hire a physician specifically because they refuse to sign an unenforceable clause, they may have a case for unfair hiring practices.[70] Whether or not it would ever be worth the time to pursue this litigation is another question.

How much should I be concerned about the language in a confidentiality agreement or NDA?

This a complicated question to answer since it depends on the position of the physician and the nature of the work involved. If the physician is involved in research, development, or technology, they will want to take a much closer look at the restrictions in the agreement. If the wording seems too broad or appears nonconfidential and confidential information could easily be mixed, a conversation and modification of the agreement should occur before signing. If the language suggests that the employer is just trying to protect their patient lists and any trade secrets, it can often be left alone. It all depends on the circumstance and possible restrictions in the state.

I have a moonlighting position or would like to take on another job. Can I do this under my contract?

A physician will need to look for exclusivity and non-competition provisions in the contract to determine if and how a physician might be able to accept a moonlighting job while employed under a contract. If one is about to accept a position, it best to have an open conversation with an employer about the moonlighting position and try to secure their approval if moonlighting it is not expressly allowed under the contract.

I have a research position or a volunteer/honorary/visiting faculty position, do I need to disclose this to my future employer?

The wording of every contract is unique. If there is an exclusivity clause, it should be reviewed carefully. Volunteer and research positions are often allowed with permission under private employment contracts. However, if the position is at a competing academic center or the employer is worried about any outside professional activities taking time away from your responsibilities in the full-time employment agreement, it might create an issue. In most situations, it is advantageous to disclose any possible conflict. A research position could also be seen as competitive if the employer is concerned about any of their proprietary information becoming intermingled in the research.

Why is there a stock sale in my contract when I am not a shareholder?

Great question. In some states that favor open policies on competition, such as a California, there is an exception to allow for non-competition agreements where there is a sale of stock. Sometimes, employers will try to sneak a non-competition agreement into a contract by using a sham stock sale.[71] Physicians should be careful about sham stock sales or any language in the contract that is trying to make it look like the contract fits into an exception for non-compete agreements where they are not allowed. A physician's contract should always conform to the reality of the position and circumstances. This applies not only to work hours, pay, and benefits but also status within the medical corporation. Unless a physician is actually becoming a shareholder, this type of language should not be included in the contract.

If I compete with my former employer, can they take away post-employment benefits?

The rules for clawback provisions vary from state to state. Each physician should consult with an expert on their state law regarding such a clause in their contract. For example, if one sees a clause in their contract that states they are forfeiting their right to further bonuses, collections, or certain pension and retirement benefits if they go work for a competitor, the physician should check the applicable state law. In California, courts have rejected attempts to circumvent the policy for open competition by using post-employment forfeiture clauses in employment agreements.[72] Again, just because they have been found by the courts to be unenforceable doesn't mean they don't show up in contracts.

In other states, this type of post-employment forfeiture clause can be considered a reasonable means of restricting competition, and the clauses may even be held to a lower legal standard than a full non-competition agreement. The jurisdictions that enforce post-termination "forfeiture" clauses do so on the theory that the former employee has a choice whether to accept the post-termination benefits or not.[73]

My contract states that I can stay on as a consultant for my former employer for a year. Does this mean I cannot compete with them during this time?

This is a fairly common arrangement in physician contracts, and it is functionally a non-compete that can be legitimate even in a state like California. Under this type of arrangement, the employee agrees to stay on as a paid consultant for a specified period as long as they do not go work for a competitor. The former employer would then have an option of whether to get paid by the former employer or work for a competitor. This agreement should be structured such that it is voluntary for the employee to enter and leave the arrangement.

My contract says it is governed by the laws of a different state than the state where the position is located. Can I be held to the covenants of a different state? What if my employer is based in another state that allows non-compete agreements?

Choice of law provisions are sometimes included in a contract to try to assert the laws of another jurisdiction. Employers include such clauses to assert the laws of another state that are more favorable for the employer. This is called "forum shopping." Whether this is allowed varies state to state. Most often an employer will forum shop for laws favorable to the employer when it comes to restrictions on competition and non-solicitation. California courts have held that if one is working in California, they are subject to a California's strong public policy on open competition.[74] This is true whether they signed the contract in California or another state. Contracts signed in California should be governed by California law, and courts decline to allow "forum shopping" in cases that involve questions of non-competition agreements.[75] Other states allow forum shopping and allow the parties to the contract to avail themselves to the laws of any jurisdiction they choose. Doctors should be very careful when signing contracts that are based in jurisdictions outside of where they live/work. If there is a contract dispute, it may mean that the parties would have to travel to that jurisdiction to be heard in court, and they may lose some protections from the law in the jurisdiction they live and work in the chosen forum.

So, if a provision is unenforceable, I can leave it in my contract then, right?

No, a physician should not leave a provision in their contract just because they believe it to be unenforceable. First, employers may leave an unenforceable provision in a contract to try to guilt or strong-arm the physician into complying with the provision. A person may change their behavior if they are aware the contract says they cannot do something, even though it may not be legally correct. Second, unfortunately, a physician could end up bound by a provision they assumed was unenforceable. If there is an arbitration provision in the contract, a physician may never see the inside of a courtroom. Arbitrators are not judges, but their decisions are final. They are not bound by the same appeals process as judges are in a court of law. State law varies, but it is often difficult to have an employment case moved from arbitration to a courtroom on appeal. If an arbitrator wrongfully upholds all or part of the non-competition agreement, the employee could be out of luck unless they take the chance to violate it and let the other party sue them in court. Please see Chapter 15 on "Dispute Resolution" to learn more about Arbitration.

Key Concepts:

- Inventions, Copyrights, Trademarks, and Patents
- Employer's Rights to Intellectual Property
- Ownership and Documentation of Inventions
- Apps, Medical Devices, and Side Projects

13. Intellectual Property

In broad terms for physician contract purposes, intellectual property rights cover inventions, research, and ideas through copyrights, patents, and trademarks. If a physician believes they need intellectual property protection, it is imperative that they speak to an intellectual property attorney. There are also many books available that provide an in-depth understanding of this area of law.

> Sample Contract Language:
>
> "Any intellectual property, ownership rights, and profit generated from intellectual property of any kind created by Physician with use of Medical Group or Hospitals property or during the work hours of Physician, including but not limited to inventions, patents, copyrights, and software, shall be considered the intellectual property of the Employer."

Most contracts contain protections for confidential information, trade secrets, and intellectual property. Intellectual Property Agreements, sometimes titled "Proprietary Information Agreements," can be included in a contract as a single paragraph or attached as a separate twenty-page addendum. Academic and research institutions often have separate intellectual property agreements to cover a wider breadth of circumstances and claim new intellectual property. Intellectual property clauses must be carefully reviewed and contain the proper language for an exception for personal inventions. Independent contractor status will not help a physician claim an invention as their own.

Employer's Rights to Intellectual Property

There are many ways employers can claim ownership of the intellectual property of an employee that has been developed while someone is employed. The most common is using the "works for hire" basis. Under the "works for hire" basis, if a work is prepared by an employee within the scope of their employment, it will likely be found to be owned by the employer.[76] If a work is prepared by an independent contractor as a commissioned work under an express agreement, it will also likely be owned by the person that commissioned the work.[77] This is a gross oversimplification of these rules, but it gives a general idea of the theory.

Employee's Rights to Intellectual Property

The law expressly limits an employer's right to demand ownership over an employee's personal inventions.[78] In simple terms, inventions must be conceived and designed on employees' own time AND without the use of employer's equipment or trade secrets to qualify for this protection. Ideally, these limitations should be expressly stated in an intellectual property agreement within a contract or added as an addendum. Additionally, a physician should always carefully document time spent working on their own inventions and seek the assistance of an intellectual property attorney when appropriate.

If you are concerned about intellectual property rights, please seek out the assistance of an intellectual property attorney. It is best to consult with a professional early on in the process of inventing or researching something that may need copyright, patent, or trademark protection.

Key Concepts:

- What is included in the contract?
- Promises discussed, but not in the final contract

14. Integration

An integration clause often noted in a contract as an Entire Agreement Clause, is a very short and simple section of the contract that is extraordinarily important.

Sample Contract Language:

"This Agreement contains the complete expression of the rights and obligations of the Parties and shall supersede all other agreements, oral and written, which were previously made by the parties. This Agreement shall not be modified, amended, or supplemented, except in a written instrument executed by both Parties."

This is the shortest chapter in the book, but maybe one of the most important. When a physician signs a final contract, the discussions they have had—offer letters, LOUs, MOUs, email promises, etc.—no longer matter unless the promises are documented in the final contract. The only thing that is legally binding is the final contract and any documents that are referenced into or attached to the final contract.

An integration clause explained simply:

1) Is everything you discussed written in your contract?

2) If not, it is not part of your contract!

One real-world caveat to this is that sometimes an organization will make a promise to a physician that for whatever reason they do not want to memorialize in writing. It could be a program director offering office space or telling a physician that they will have certain perks. Or perhaps a promise from a superior that a partnership offer will happen in a year's time. This type of promise is common and the promises are not legally binding if they are not in the contract. However, if the physician has enough of a relationship with the person making the promises, they can choose to overlook this and put their trust in that person. This is a very personal decision in each individual situation.

Common Questions

I have everything documented in an email, is it OK that it is not in the final contract?

As stated above, if it is not in the final contract, it is not part of the agreement. An employer may choose to uphold promises that have been made and are not memorialized in the contract, but it would be very difficult for a physician to force the employer to uphold such promises.

The LOU spells everything out, but the contract does not contain a lot of detail, does it need to be in the final contract?

Once the contract is signed, the LOU is not meaningful. The LOU is a precursor to the contract, not a part of the final agreement.

I was told it is an oral agreement or gentleman's agreement, is that OK?

To ensure enforceability, promises should be memorialized in writing. Oral agreements are enforceable under some circumstances in certain states. However, for the many reasons detailed in this book a physician should always have a written contract. The contract should not be a hybrid of oral and written promises because if there is a written contract, it is hard to make the argument that an additional oral contract also existed.

Key Concepts:

- Alternative Dispute Resolution
- Arbitration Clause and Process
- Pros and Cons of Arbitration Clauses

15. Arbitration and Dispute Resolution

There are many different types of dispute resolution; going to court is not the only venue for a contract dispute. Alternative Dispute Resolution (ADR) has grown significantly over the last couple of decades. ADR includes formal Mediation and Arbitration of claims. Mediation is a less formal type of dispute resolution and in many cases involves a third party trying to help the parties sort out the issues and come to an amicable solution. If Mediation fails, Arbitration is a way of handling more complex disputes outside of the court system.[79] There is also an arbitration system within the court system called Judicial Arbitration. Some contracts use arbitration as the first line of defense, and others exhaust other mediation methods first and are specific about the parameters for an arbitration.

Sample Contract Language:

"Parties agree to use good faith negotiations to resolve any dispute, claim, or controversy that may arise under this agreement. In the event that the parties are unable to resolve any dispute, the matter will be presented before a formal mediator. If mediation is unsuccessful, the dispute will be settled in arbitration in accordance with the arbitration laws of this state. The parties accept the arbitrator's award as final and binding."

Sample Arbitration Process

1. Written notice identifying and describing the nature of all claims asserted is provided by one party.
2. An Arbitrator hears the case and issues a written opinion describing the findings.
3. Either party can appeal the Arbitrator's opinion within a set amount of time depending on the rules governing the arbitration.
4. The Arbitrator will then consider the issues and either confirm or change the decision, which will be final and binding on both parties.

It seems common to sign an arbitration agreement for almost everything now, but a physician should know the consequences of signing such an agreement and how such a clause can affect their rights and professional practice in the future. Arbitration agreements vary greatly in their scope and structure. Most agreements attempt to be comprehensive and cover all claims except those restricted by law.

Many agreements are binding, mandatory, and ask the physician to waive the right to have a jury trial or seek remedy from the court system. This means that an employee may be signing away the right to have their case heard in front of a jury that might be more sympathetic to the case than an arbitrator. Arbitration agreements may also ask a physician to waive the right to file a class action lawsuit against an employer. This means only individual claims can be brought to an arbitrator, thereby negating the ability to combine cases with other physicians who may have been similarly wronged.

Arbitration and Privacy

One of the often-cited benefits is that arbitration protects the privacy of all parties involved since arbitration rulings are not entered into the public record. This is particularly important for physicians since there may be private patient information or data that could be exposed. On the other side of this, it can also allow a company to settle individually and privately with many people for the same claim.

Potential Drawbacks

In an arbitration, the Arbitrator has the final word, even if it does not adhere to the letter of the law.[80] For some disputes, arbitration can create an easier and more cost-effective resolution to a contractual dispute. Other times, it would be helpful to have the ear and sympathy of a jury and appeals process to gain a more favorable resolution in a case. It is also important to take into account that employers may have more leverage in arbitration than employees. This is particularly true when an employer does a lot of arbitrations as they may use the same person as an arbitrator. An arbitrator is supposed to be completely neutral and unbiased, but in practice that is not always the case. It is also not as cost-effective to go through arbitration instead of a court as many people think.

Common Questions

The arbitration agreement in my contract says that I cannot be part of a class-action? Is that OK?

As discussed above, many companies are adding in protection against class action lawsuits into their arbitration clauses. This issue is increasingly being argued in courts as to whether this is a legal restraint or provides too much shelter and protection for large companies found to be involved in widespread fraud schemes. If you can request the removal of such a clause, it would be best, but that is not always practical.

I've heard arbitration clauses are beneficial and save time and money. Should I request the addition of an arbitration clause?

The big picture idea of arbitration is that it will provide a good and fair result for all parties with less cost and formality than a traditional court hearing. While this is true some of the time, the system is not perfect, and many plaintiff employment lawyers tell clients that it is better for the employee to be in the court system to resolve employment disputes. Sometimes this has to do with the amount of discovery time and access to files that one might receive in arbitration versus in a court. At some level, it is a personal choice, but it is certainly not always advisable to add in such a clause if the employer is not requesting an arbitration clause. It is best to talk to an attorney in the applicable state to determine the best course of action for each contract.

There is a clause in my contract that is technically unenforceable, should I leave it in my contract?

A physician should not allow a legally unenforceable clause to remain in their contract even knowing that it is unenforceable. An example of this is signing an agreement containing an unenforceable non-competition clause. As stated above, one of the reasons is that in court and arbitrations, the final judgments do not always comply exactly to the letter of the law. In court, if a verdict does not comply with the law, one can appeal the verdict and receive a new trial. However, there can be significant added expense and hassle to appeal and go through a new trial. In arbitration, in many states, it can be very difficult to appeal a ruling.

Key Concepts:

- Indemnification and "Hold Harmless" Clauses
- Impact of the Clauses and Standards of Negligence
- Indemnification for Billing Errors
- Negotiating Changes in the Clauses

16. Indemnification and "Hold Harmless" Clauses

Indemnification means one or both parties agree to take financial responsibility for losses stemming from acts or omissions on behalf of the other party.[81] A "hold harmless" clause is similar in that one party is assuming liability and releasing the other party from liability.[82] Some contracts contain very broad and one-sided indemnification and "hold harmless" clauses favoring the drafter who is usually the employer. When such a clause is present, it is advisable not to sign the contract until the clause has been thoroughly reviewed and modified to ensure the physician is not taking on too much risk by signing the contract.

Sample Contract Language:

Physician as Indemnifying Party:

"To the extent not inconsistent with applicable law or covered by insurance of Employer, Physician agrees to defend, indemnify, and hold Employer harmless from and against any and all claims, expenses or liability, including reasonable attorney's fees and costs, relating to or arising out of any grossly negligent or reckless actions or omission of Physician during the term of Physician's employment with the Employer resulting in an Employer's liability to a third party."

Employer as Indemnifying Party:

"Except as covered by insurance, Group shall indemnify and hold harmless Physician for all acts or omissions within the scope of employment. Where Physician is found to be grossly negligent or acting outside of the scope of employment, Physician agrees to indemnify and hold harmless Group for all damages and fees related to Physician's grossly negligent acts or omissions."

This type of clause is relevant when discussing contract disputes between the employer and physician and when discussing negligent or criminal actions of an employee, often in the context of malpractice claims. For the employee, the narrower the clause, the better. Broad clauses can open up physicians to liability. However, these clauses can work both ways. In an employment context, physicians should always seek to be broadly indemnified by their employers. As an independent contractor, whether the clause should be broad or narrow is more open to interpretation based on the nature of the work and how much control the contractor has versus the employer. If a physician is asked by a health system to take a position that might involve personal financial risk, for example, opening a new low-income clinic, they can ask to be fully indemnified for the financial risk involved even as an independent contractor.

The Rationale for Indemnification of Physicians

In many states, including California, an employer is responsible for indemnifying an employee for losses related to events occurring within the scope of employment.[83] In such states, an employee should not be personally liable for things that happened while they were on official business or within the control of their employer. A physician, whether an employee or independent contractor, may be asked to indemnify an employer if the employee's actions or omissions are found to be negligent or grossly negligent and outside the scope of employment.

Hospitals and Groups are assumed to have much more money and assets than an individual physician. As a result, larger judgments are generally awarded when a health care entity is sued as opposed to an individual. If a physician is responsible for indemnifying a hospital system, it could have significant financial consequences for the physician to pay attorney fees, damages, and costs of litigation on behalf of the institution. Malpractice will not protect a physician from the financial consequences of this type of clause, and in some cases, such a clause may prevent a physician from taking advantage of their malpractice because they have contracted to assume liability.[84] If a broad clause stating the physician will indemnify the hospital is contained in a contract, one should consider requesting removal. If the employer insists on keeping it intact, it is wise to change the standard to state that the physician is only liable to indemnify the employer in cases where they are grossly negligent or acted in "bad faith," a concept which is discussed in the next section. It is my experience that the individuals who ask physicians to sign these contracts often do not understand the possible ramifications of such a clause on an individual physician.

Reckless or Grossly Negligent Actions of Physician

Many contracts contain provisions stating that if a physician is grossly negligent or reckless, they will have to indemnify the entity for any costs associated with the behavior. Gross negligence or recklessness are often described as actions that are outside the acceptable norms of society that they shock the conscience. This type of clause is usually reasonable but must be read carefully. Physicians should avoid signing something that states they have an indemnification obligation for being merely negligent, not grossly negligent. The negligence standard is generally too broad and could lead to too much liability for an individual physician. As with all provisions, it is best to check with a professional in the applicable state since the law does vary from state to state.

Indemnification and Billing

A broad billing indemnification clause such as the one below can open a physician up to liability for fraud claims.

> Sample Contract Language:
>
> "This indemnification obligation of Physician shall extend to, without limitation, any claim relating to billing errors or omissions."

Physicians have a responsibility to bill accurately. Legally the consequences of inaccurate billing ultimately lie with the physician. Therefore, if there are other people involved in submitting and processing billing who are not the physician's direct employees, the physician should be indemnified by the employer for mistakes and false claims attributed to their employees.

All physicians should make sure they have full control or oversight of billing and double check everything to make sure there are no false claims under their name and license. False claims are discussed in more detail in the next chapter about anti-fraud laws.

Common Questions

How to modify these clauses?

As with most requests to modify the contract, the first step is to ask for revision, possibly offering revised language for the employer's consideration. Sometimes, this is all it takes to modify the clause. Other times modifying an indemnification clause in a contract can be difficult. If the employer has an attorney, it is usually best for counsel to speak to each other to make a quick modification or discuss the rationale behind a specific clause. If the employer does not have an attorney and does not fully understand the clause, they may not grasp the significance of the change. This clause can create some tension between the parties. Each situation will be different, and it is best to speak to counsel in the jurisdiction of the contract.

How important are these clauses?

As discussed above, if the physician is on the hook for a judgment against a hospital, it could be a very significant financial obligation that may bankrupt the physician. It is important for these clauses to be fair and not one-sided. This can be a challenging area of the contract to understand and communicate to the employer, but it should not be overlooked just because it is complicated.

Key Concepts:

- False Claims Act
- Anti-Kickback Statute
- Stark Law (Physician Self-Referral Law)
- Exception and Safe Harbor Provisions
- Exclusion Statute

17. Anti-Fraud Laws

THIS SECTION INTRODUCES THE BASIC CONCEPTS OF A FEW FEDERAL LAWS FOR EDUCATIONAL PURPOSES ONLY. VARIATIONS IN STATE LAW ARE NOT ADDRESSED. THE INFORMATION PRESENTED HERE IS SIMPLIFIED AND SHOULD NOT BE APPLIED DIRECTLY TO ANY INDIVIDUAL SITUATION.

Anti-fraud laws in medicine are ever evolving and create quite a complicated web of procedures and rules that must be followed. There are laws against false claims either in the form of fraudulent billing or billing by a person that is not a licensed professional. There are also laws against self-dealing and accepting kickbacks that have developed to protect patients against harm and to try to slow down increases in health care costs due to fraudulent activity.[85] This chapter will discuss a few of these laws and provide a brief overview of some of the requirements and penalties.

As the above disclaimer suggests, this is an area of law that is extremely complicated and requires each contract and situation to be analyzed on its own merits. This section introduces the key concepts of each law and explains why it is important to make sure a contract is compliant. This section does not give a rubric to follow to analyze an individual contract. At the very end of this chapter, there is a summary of a few things a physician can look for in their contract to spot red flags, but again, this is not comprehensive and should not be taken as such.

The discussion below will refer to "safe harbors" and "exceptions" within certain laws. A "safe harbor" is a way for individuals to proactively comply with a law and meet certain requirements so that if there ever is a problem, the intent to comply will be shown by the contract and actions of the individuals involved.[86] Compliance with a safe harbor is voluntary and not always possible. Even if a safe harbor cannot be met, the actions may not be illegal, though they may fall within the grey area of the law. An "exception" means that the conduct of the parties or the agreement violates the law and there is an "exception" carved into the law to allow for certain business relationships.[87] Exceptions must be followed, or the parties will violate the law.

The terms "bona fide employee" and "personal services" or "professional services" will also be used below. Generally, when looking at physician contracts, a "bona fide employee" contract is what we think of as a traditional employment relationship, and a "personal or professional services" contract refers to an independent contractor agreement.

False Claims Act

The False Claims Act (FCA) is a law that among other things, states it is illegal to submit claims for payment to Medicare or Medicaid that one knows or should know are fraudulent.[88] The FCA permits recovery of funds from anyone who knowingly presents or causes to be presented a fraudulent claim for payment to the government. To establish FCA liability, it must be proven that a defendant knowingly submitted or caused to be submitted a false claim for reimbursement of services. The claim need not be entirely fraudulent to violate the FCA. Rather, the FCA prohibits the use of any false statement or document in support of a claim for government funds.[89] Billing for procedures that did not occur or were unnecessary can also be a false claim.[90]

It is important for a physician to have a clear understanding of to whom they are assigning the right to bill and collect for services under their contract and how billing will occur. In many situations, when a physician works for a group or hospital system, they submit their billing and then may not have much oversight over the final billing. Even without oversight, a physician is generally considered to be liable for what is billed under their name and license. Some contracts even have indemnification clauses asking a physician to indemnify the hospital for any wrongfully billed items, not just errors in their own billing submissions. Physicians should take an active role in understanding the billing procedures and the people responsible for them. Assignment of the right to the bill is discussed further in Chapter 19.

Currently, the fines for violating the FCA can be up to $11,000 per claim filed and three times the amount improperly claimed. These penalties continue to change, and each billed item can be counted as a separate claim, so these fines and penalties can add up quickly.[91] There are also criminal claims under this act which can lead to possible jail time.[92]

Anti-Kickback Statute (AKS)

Kickbacks in popular nomenclature generally refer to illicit payments or improper payments to a person that is in a position of power to make the obtained income or future income possible.[93] In health care, kickbacks have a similar definition with some concrete rules and guidelines found in the Anti-Kickback Statute (AKS). Kickbacks in health care can include splitting fees, payments for referrals, and even gifts provided by an employer to an employee. AKS is a criminal and civil statute that prohibits knowing and willful "remuneration" to induce or reward patient referrals or generation of business involving an item or service payable by Medicare or Medicaid.[94] Items payable by Medicare and Medicaid, include drugs, supplies, services, etc. Remuneration includes anything of value and can take the form of anything of value including cash, and things such as free rent, expensive meals or hotel stays, and excessive compensation.[95] As described below, remuneration does not include any amount paid by an employer to an employee, who has a bona fide employment relationship with the employer. The referrals must be for furnishing of any item or service for which payment may be made in whole or in part under Medicare, Medicaid, or other Federal health care programs.

AKS is not a strict liability statute like Stark Law, which means the actions leading to a violation of the statute must be knowingly undertaken. However, AKS can be violated if even one purpose of an agreement is to induce referrals. Health care providers can make referrals that do not violate the Anti-Kickback Statute by structuring their arrangements to fit within an exception or "safe harbor" in the Statute that exempts certain referral arrangements from its prohibitions. The "safe harbors" provide a legal defense to those accused of violating the statute and compliance is not always possible. The most commonly used exceptions and safe harbor provisions in physician employment and independent contractor agreements are below.

AKS Exceptions and Safe Harbors

Personal Services Safe Harbor[96]

1. The agreement is set out in writing and signed by the parties;
2. The agreement covers all of the services the agent provides to the principal for the term of the agreement and specifies the services to be provided by the agent;
3. If the agreement is intended to provide for the services of the agent on a periodic, sporadic or part-time basis, rather than on a full-time basis for the term of the agreement, the agreement specifies exactly the schedule of such intervals, their precise length, and the exact charge for such intervals;
4. The term of the agreement is for not less than one year;
5. The aggregate compensation paid to the agent over the term of the agreement is set in advance, is consistent with fair market value in arms-length transactions and is not determined in a manner that takes into account the volume or value of any referrals or business otherwise

generated between the parties for which payment may be made in whole or in part under Medicare, Medicaid or other Federal health care programs;

6. The services performed under the agreement do not involve the counseling or promotion of a business arrangement or other activity that violates any State or Federal law; and
7. The aggregate services contracted for do not exceed those which are reasonably necessary to accomplish the commercially reasonable business purpose of the services.

Bona Fide Employee Exception[97]

The definition of "remuneration" excludes "any amount paid by an employer to an employee, who has a bona fide employment relationship with the employer, for employment in the provision of covered items or services." Covered items or services are those for which payment may be made in whole or in part under Medicare, Medicaid or other Federal health care programs.

Stark Law (Physician Self-Referral Law)

Stark Law provides that when a physician (or immediate family member) has a financial relationship with an entity where "designated health services" are performed, the physician may not make a referral for which payment will be made under Medicare or Medicaid.

The following are common questions about Stark Law and are taken directly from starklaw.org in February 2019. Please check the site for relevant updates.

Who is an immediate family member?

The term "immediate family member" is defined broadly to mean a husband or wife; birth or adoptive parent, child or sibling; stepparent, stepchild, stepbrother, or stepsister; father-in-law, mother-in-law, son-in-law, daughter-in-law, brother-in-law, or sister-in-law;

grandparent or grandchild; and spouse of a grandparent or grandchild.[98]

What constitutes a financial relationship?

A "financial relationship" is defined to include either a direct or indirect ownership or investment interest in an entity through equity, debt or other means, or a direct or indirect compensation arrangement with an entity.[99]

What are designated health services?

The Designated Health Services (DHS) encompassed within Stark include the following categories:

- clinical laboratory services;
- physical therapy services;
- occupational therapy and speech-language pathology services;
- radiology services, including nuclear medicine, MRI, CAT scans, and ultrasound services;
- radiation therapy services and supplies;
- durable medical equipment and supplies;
- parenteral and enteral nutrients, equipment and supplies;
- prosthetics, orthotics, and prosthetic devices and supplies;
- home health services;
- outpatient prescription drugs; and
- inpatient and outpatient hospitalization services

With regard to the first five categories of DHS, the Stark regulations identify the specific insurance billing codes in each category, which are considered to constitute DHS. The remaining six categories of DHS are defined in the Stark regulatory text.[100]

What is a referral?

Stark broadly defines "referral" to include a request by a physician for an item or service payable under Medicare or Medicaid (including the request by a physician for consultation with another physician and any test or procedure ordered or performed by such other physician), or a request by a physician for the establishment of a plan of care that includes the provision of a DHS. The definition of "referral" does not include services personally performed by a referring/ordering physician (but not services furnished by employees or other members of the same group practice as the ordering physician). Accordingly, physicians who personally perform the DHS that they order for their patients can structure arrangements without worrying about potential Stark violations.[101]

What are the penalties?

Penalties for violating Stark can be severe. They include denial of payment, refund of payment, the imposition of a $15,000 per service civil monetary penalty, and imposition of a $100,000 civil monetary penalty for each arrangement considered to be a circumvention scheme.[102]

Exceptions to Stark Law

It is important to note that this is what is called a strict liability statute, which means no intent is required. If a referral is made, the law is triggered, and the physician's behavior must fall within one of the exceptions to the law. Some of the most common exceptions used for Stark Law in physician contracts are:

Bona Fide Employment Exception[103]

1. The employment is for identifiable services;
2. The amount of remuneration provided under the employment relationship is consistent with Fair Market Value and is not determined in a manner that takes into account (directly or indirectly) the volume or value of referrals by the referring physician; and

3. The remuneration is provided pursuant to an agreement which would be commercially reasonable even if no referrals were made to the employer.

Personal Services Exception[104]

1. The agreement must be set out in writing and signed by both parties;
2. The agreement must cover all services to be provided;
3. If the agreement is for part-time services must specify the exact schedule of intervals, length, and exact charge/payment;
4. The term must not be for less than one year;
5. The aggregate compensation paid over the term of the agreement set in advance, consistent with a Fair Market Value arm's length transaction;
6. The agreement does not take into account the volume or value of referrals or business otherwise generated between the parties for services billed to federal programs;
7. There are no other laws are violated by the agreement; and
8. The aggregate services contracted for do not exceed those reasonably necessary to accomplish the commercially reasonable purpose of the contract.

Group Practice Exception[105]

There are often referral arrangements within group practices that technically violate Stark Law. Groups can carefully structure their arrangements to fit into the Group Practice Exception of Stark Law. The group practice exception should be carefully reviewed to ensure the requirements are met, including the type of business, number of physicians in the practice, scope of services provided, accounting practices, profit sharing, and other requirements of this section of Stark Law.

Exclusion Statute

The Office of Inspector General (OIG) is legally required to exclude from participation in all Federal health care programs individuals and entities convicted of the following types of criminal offenses:

1. Medicare or Medicaid fraud, as well as any other offenses related to the delivery of items or services under Medicare or Medicaid;
2. patient abuse or neglect;
3. felony convictions for other healthcare-related fraud, theft, or other financial misconduct; and
4. felony convictions for unlawful manufacture, distribution, prescription, or dispensing of controlled substances.[106]

According to their site, the OIG has the "discretion to exclude individuals and entities on several other grounds, including misdemeanor convictions related to health care fraud other than Medicare or Medicaid fraud or misdemeanor convictions in connection with the unlawful manufacture, distribution, prescription, or dispensing of controlled substances; suspension, revocation, or surrender of a license to provide health care for reasons bearing on professional competence, professional performance, or financial integrity; provision of unnecessary or substandard services; submission of false or fraudulent claims to a Federal health care program; engaging in unlawful kickback arrangements; and defaulting on health education loan or scholarship obligations."[107]

This means if a physician is excluded by OIG from participation in the Federal healthcare programs, then Medicare, Medicaid, and other Federal health care programs, such as TRICARE and the Veterans Health Administration, will not pay for items or services that they furnish, order, or prescribe. Excluded physicians may not bill directly for treating Medicare and Medicaid patients, nor may their services be billed indirectly through an employer or a group practice. In addition, if they furnish services to a patient on a private-pay basis, no order or prescription that they give to that patient will be reimbursable by any Federal health care program.[108]

Common Questions

Do physicians need to worry about these laws? Don't they usually go after the employer if there is a problem?

It used to be the case that most of the onus was on employers and larger organizations. However, more and more physicians need to be cognizant of these laws as individual physicians are targets of fraud actions from the Office of Inspector General. In 2015, there was a memo written by acting Attorney General Sally Yates that made it clear that individual physicians should be on notice that their actions, pay, and contracts are under scrutiny. In the last few years, there has been an uptick in the number of fraud claims brought against physicians.[109]

I am buying in as a partner to a surgery center where I will send referrals, is this OK under Stark Law?

It can be, yes, but it is best to talk with a health care compliance attorney and make sure that the referrals are properly handled before investing in such a center.

My company throws a big party every year for its employees and provides other benefits, are these kickbacks?

There are exceptions for some events under the Anti-Kickback Statute. Events that benefit all employees are generally OK as long as the reporting rules are followed. Also, there is a nominal gift amount of a few hundred dollars that is an exception under the statute.

What happens if I am excluded from billing under federal programs?

It is a very big problem for a physician to be excluded from federal programs. It means that they cannot bill Medicare or Medicaid. Being able to bill for medical services under Federal programs is a condition for many positions as a physician. Speak to a medical practice attorney if there is ever a chance you will be excluded from billing to federal programs.

This all sounds very complicated. I understand I should seek out professional help for a specific employment contract question, but are there a few things to look out for as red flags?

To comply with anti-fraud laws, most physician contracts should be:

1. In writing;
2. Signed by both parties;
3. For at least one year;
4. Cover all services to be provided;
5. Compensation set in advance;
6. Consistent with Fair Market Value;
7. Compensation does not take into account the volume or value of referrals or business generated between parties; and
8. Services contracted for are reasonable

Please note, this list is not inclusive, and again should not be taken as legal advice as to any specific contract; however, if any of these points are missing from the contract, it would be wise to seek out counsel.

Key Concepts:

- Due Process Rights and Hospital Privileges
- Protection for Physicians
- Waiver of Protections by Physicians

18. Hospital Privileges and Due Process

Though most physicians do not think about their hospital privileges as anything more than their ability to work in a given hospital, privileges can play an important role in a physician's ability to practice medicine and maintain their reputation. Once hospital privileges are granted by the bylaws of almost all hospitals, they cannot be involuntarily terminated without a peer review process and a hearing.[110] The right created is referred to as a due process right, meaning that there must be a formal process to take it away without consent.[111] The process typically includes a formal hearing in front of a peer review board where the physician has the opportunity to defend themselves and refute the allegations. When this right remains intact, a physician may sue a hospital for breach of contract if privileges are removed or restricted without the required due process.

Sample Contract language:

"If Physician's employment relationship with the Practice is terminated for any reason whatsoever, the privileges of Physician at the hospital or any other health care facilities to which he or she is assigned will terminate automatically, and Physician expressly waives any right to any challenge or review (under any fair hearing plan or

> otherwise) of the termination of his or her Privileges at the hospital or at those health care facilities and all claims of any kind whatsoever, including due process claims, he or she or his or her estate may have against the Practice or any of its affiliates and all other parties with respect to the termination of his or her Privileges."

The due process right in hospital privileges stems from the Health Care Quality Improvement Act of 1986 and has been affirmed by the Joint Commission, which accredits and certifies health care organizations and programs around the country.[112] Interestingly physicians with due process rights are more likely to bring attention to fraudulent practices that threaten the integrity of the Medicare and Medicaid programs. They are also more likely to act in the best interest of the patient without fear of retribution from their employer.[113]

Waiver of Due Process Rights and Termination of Privileges

Physicians are often asked as a term of their employment to obtain hospital admitting privileges and staff privileges at least one hospital. Many contracts, especially for large private groups, ask the physician to waive their right to peer review and a hearing before the termination of privileges. This is done to alleviate administrative burdens on the group and hospital involved and allow the hospital or group to terminate a physician with less hassle and process. If a physician waives their right to a hearing, they could end up being fired on the spot, being terminated for something that they believe is an erroneous reason, or even being wrongfully accused of a crime that could jeopardize their ability to practice medicine in the future. When peer review hearings are afforded, the physician can defend themselves among their peers instead of at the mercy of an administrator.

A scenario under which a hearing may be necessary is one where a physician has been accused of doing something to recklessly injure a patient, using illegal drugs, or another significant breach of their ethical duty as a physician. If there is a good reason to involuntarily strip a physician of their privileges for certain adverse actions, it may trigger a mandatory reporting requirement to the State

Medical Board and the National Practitioners Database (NPDB), which could stay on a physician's record for a long time.[114] In addition, if privileges are suspended for a significant amount of time or a voluntary resignation or termination occurred after notification of an impending investigation, this reporting requirement can also be triggered.[115] If these agencies are notified, the results can create trouble for the physician when applying for a new position or even create an inability to continue to practice medicine if the violations are significant enough. Had a physician not waived their right to a hearing, they would have had a chance to adjudicate the claim in front of a panel of their peers and potentially not have had their privileges revoked in the first place. For this reason, there is a movement among regulators, physician advocates, and professional groups to stop the practice of full waivers of due process rights.[116]

Common Question

How can I protect myself against a waiver of Due Process right in a contract?

Very simply, do not waive your due process right to a hearing before losing your hospital privileges. A waiver can be phrased in the contract in a number of different ways, but if the contract says you are waiving your right to a hearing or peer review before your privileges can be terminated or you can be fired, think carefully and speak to an attorney before signing your contract.

Key Concepts:

- Standards for Physicians in Practice
- Warranties of Physician
- Billing, Assignment, and Collection of Fees
- Notice Provisions
- Medical Records

19. Miscellaneous Contract Provisions

Professionalism, Ethics, and Moral Standards

Most physician contracts contain a section stating the physician must practice within the appropriate professional and ethical standard of care of the community in a particular specialty. This wording generally allows for regional differences in practice while holding physicians to a high standard. When a position is with a group or hospital with a religious affiliation, the physician may be asked to comply with certain moral standards usually contained in employee handbooks. It is important to fully understand all of the obligations the contract is placing on the physician, so there are no surprises later. Contracts may require committee involvement, social obligations in the medical community, and attending events to boost the reputation of the employer. If there is something in the contract that a physician cannot or is unwilling to comply with, they should always speak to the employer before signing the agreement.

Warranties

There is often a section regarding material representations of the physician under which the physician is asked to disclose any malpractice or other legal claims against them or their medical license. The section may also request physicians disclose any discipline by the medical board or even formal discipline by a former employer or training institution. This section should be read carefully, and if there are necessary disclosures, the physician should speak to counsel about how to disclose it to the employer.

Billing and Assignment of Professional Fees

Employment contracts almost always provide that all rights to collect fees and bill are assigned to the employer or contracting entity unless another arrangement is present. This means that the employer will have the right to bill under the physician's license and directly collect all fees for providing medical care on their behalf. The employer then compensates the physician based on the agreed compensation arrangement in the contract. A physician employee should submit accurate and complete billing information in connection with all professional medical services rendered by the physician. The physician can be asked to clarify billing information and provide detailed notes on the patient encounter in order to assist with the employer's efforts to collect and ensure proper billing. However, a physician should not be required to assist in the direct collection of fees if the physician has assigned the right to bill and collect to the employer or contracting entity.

Notice Provisions

Notice provisions are an often overlooked section of a contract. It is important to make sure all of the contact information under this section is current as it will be the official address for each party to the contract. If a physician provides notice about their contract, it should comply with the requirements of this section. Notice is particularly important when a physician wishes to terminate the contract, provide notice of an anticipated leave, or notify an employer of a pending malpractice claim. Compliance with such a section may mean sending a hard copy letter of resignation to the CEO of the hospital or group or providing notice to multiple people for any requested change to the contract. If notice is not properly provided under the terms of the contract, the employer can refuse to accept the notice as of the original date until it is given under the terms of the agreement.

Medical Records

Medical records are an important part of modern medical practice. They serve as a record for treating physicians, groups, insurance companies, and other legal obligations of the physician and employer. Ownership and access to medical records are often mentioned in contracts for physician services. Most often, a group or hospital will claim ownership of medical records. Physicians should always make sure they have appropriate access to records while they are employed and after if there is a legal action that requires them to access the records.

Common Questions

Is notification in person or email OK?

Generally, no. Review the notice section of the contract to properly provide notice for any change to the contract or to offer a resignation. If the contract allows for communication by email for this purpose, then it would be acceptable. Notice is usually always required in writing, so giving notice only in person will likely fall short of the requirements. It is nice to have a personal conversation, but the conversation should be followed up with formal written notice in compliance with the requirements of the specific contract.

My contract states that I will attend social events, is this reasonable?

Attending social and professional events is reasonable to a certain extent. If the requirements of this type of provision in a contract impede on the physician's life outside of work, it is possible it has crossed over the line into work hours. Always inquire about the expectations and requirements of this type of clause in a contract.

My contract states I will help with billing collections, but I thought I assigned away my rights to bill for services. Is this OK?

No. If a physician has assigned the right to bill to the employer, they should not be asked to help directly with billing collection from patients. It is appropriate, however, for the billing staff to ask a physician questions about their notes or require a physician finish providing billing information for a patient to bill and collect from the patient.

PART FIVE

20. Recruitment, Relocation, and Guaranteed Income Agreements

Recruitment, Relocation, and Guaranteed Income Agreements are used to attract doctors to accept a position with a new institution or move to a new city or state. Physicians with special skills may be recruited to move to an area and fill a need or start an innovative practice in the area. Physicians must pay attention to the details and restrictions of such an offer. Relocation agreements are also used to tempt physicians to move to an underserved area where there are not enough physicians to serve the patient population.[117] Hospitals and groups can recruit and entice physicians to come to underserved areas with higher pay and other benefits. There are rules that need to be followed to avoid liability under certain anti-fraud laws and to avoid scrutiny under a Fair Market Value determination.[118] In addition, the compensation and fringe benefits must be narrowly tailored to meet the objective of procuring a physician to serve the population in the areas.[119] Despite the risks and extra rules, hospitals in underserved areas are in such great need of physicians that they work with the regulations and offer substantial relocation packages to physicians.

Sample Contract Language:

"Hospital shall make a loan available to Physician and/or Professional Corporation consisting of the advances described in this agreement, including Income Guarantee, Moving Expenses Advance, Assistance Advance, and

> Signing Bonus. Physician and/or Professional Corporation shall repay the Recruitment Loan pursuant to the terms and conditions of the Recruitment Note; however, amounts due to Hospital under the Recruitment Note may be forgiven, in whole or in part, as applicable, if certain conditions, outlined in this agreement are satisfied by Physician or Professional Corporation."

Typical Benefits in Recruitment Agreements:

- Guaranteed Income
- Covering Business Expenses
- Reimbursing Relocation Expenses
- Signing Bonus
- Retention Bonus
- Housing Loan Assistance
- Assistance with Student Loan Payments

Income Guarantee

Under an Income Guarantee hospitals and sometimes private groups provide a recruited physician with a guaranteed income for a certain amount of time in exchange for a promise to remain in the area for a specified number of years. In a typical scenario, a hospital may agree to cover the expenses as well as the monthly compensation and benefits of the physician for a specified time. Most of the time, as the physician's revenue increases, the hospital pays less of the guarantee and pays only to make up for the difference between guarantee and revenues. The arrangement is used to entice a relocating physician by ensuring financial stability for the first year or two of the relocation. In addition to the relocation agreement, there should be a promissory note when such a contract is executed. The promissory note should state in detail the terms of the income guarantee. Generally, money is advanced as a loan and the physician must either stay in an area defined by zip codes to practice for a specified period of time or be liable to pay back the amount of income advanced in the first year. It is advisable to retain the services of an accountant to make sure all of the finances add up and obtain guidance for paying taxes on the loan amounts.

When the obligations of the physician are fulfilled, the physician should be released from the terms of the promissory note and all loans should be forgiven. Every month or year the physician works in the area is typically credited toward the loan balance. Essentially, the loan is paid off by keeping the promise to stay within the service area. If a physician is considering such a position, they should carefully consider the amount of money they are accepting and if they can fulfill the obligations of the contract. Many guaranteed income contracts contain a stipulation that if a physician breaches the contract, they can be liable for the full amount of the loan immediately. It is very important to examine the employment contract or independent contractor agreement that accompanies an income guarantee to make sure that the termination provisions are fair. If a contract is terminated, a physician may not be able to live up to their obligation to stay in the service area and could be liable to pay back the full value of the loan immediately. This can be a financial obligation larger than most physicians can handle on short notice.

Important Clauses and Considerations

Liability for Loan on Death or Permanent Disability

When a physician enters a relocation or recruitment agreement with a guaranteed income, the physician is potentially taking on a lot of liability. In the event of the physician's death or disability during the loan or forgiveness period, it is important to try to negotiate that liability does not fall on the physician's family. Liability may be shared among group partners if agreed upon or written off by the hospital.

> The inclusion of a clause such as the following is important:
>
> "Hospital shall forgive the entire outstanding principal balance of, and all accrued unpaid interest owing on, the Recruitment Note, together will all

applicable fees, costs, and charges, if any, in the event of Physician's death or Permanent Disability."

Opportunity in Area and Length of Contract

Most recruitment agreements stipulate that the physician must stay in the service area or cover a certain hospital for a defined amount of time, but not necessarily continue to work for the same employer. It is important to assess the potential for other opportunities in the area of relocation in case the anticipated position does not work out as planned.

Expense Guidelines and Reconciliation Reports

Detailed requirements for how a physician or practice must submit reconciliation reports and expense guidelines to the hospital or group providing the guaranteed income should be included in the agreements. As stated above, many guaranteed income contracts only pay a guaranteed income to cover the difference between the amount received for services and the promised salary. It is the responsibility of the physician and the practice to make sure all reports are delivered to the payee promptly. The contract should be specific about these requirements as well as provide specific time frames within which the payee will pay out the remaining loan amounts to the physician. It is advisable to seek the help of an accountant in preparing these statements and handling the tax consequences of such an arrangement.

For moving expenses or housing loans, there should be guidelines for submitting receipts, using certain companies, maximums reimbursements, and even a promise to pay back moving expenses if the physician does not stay through the contract. It is important to carefully review all parameters for such benefits. Particularly when it comes to housing loans or large loans of any kind, it is very important to get all of the appropriate details.

Anti-Fraud Laws and Relocation Agreements

Some anti-fraud laws provide guidance as to when compensation and benefits above Fair Market Value for relocation are proper.[120] These are complex agreements, and legal counsel should be obtained to review and answer questions on any particular contract and accompanying promissory notes. As was the case in the earlier chapter on Anti-Fraud laws, due to the complexity of the laws, the following is only for educational purposes to show some of the factors used to determine if it is permissible to induce the physician to relocate.

Under Stark Law, the following exceptions are written into the law to allow for some arrangements that assist hospitals and medical groups with recruiting in underserved areas:

Recruitment payments by Hospital Stark Law Exception[121]

1. The agreement must be in writing and signed by both parties;
2. Physician relocates to the hospital's geographic area;
3. 75% of revenues must be from new patients;
4. The arrangement must not be conditioned on physician's referrals of patients to the hospital;
5. The remuneration not based on the volume or value of referrals to hospital; and
6. The physician may establish privileges at other hospitals.

Recruitment payment made to a medical group Stark Law Exception[122]

1. A written agreement is also signed by the group;
2. Payment is passed directly through the group, except for actual costs, and remains with a recruited physician;
3. Costs allocated to the recruited physician do not exceed actual incremental costs attributable to the recruited physician if it is an income guarantee;
4. The records of actual costs are maintained;
5. The remuneration does not take into account the volume or value of referrals;
6. The group does not unreasonably restrict the physician's ability to practice medicine; and

7. The arrangement does not violate Anti-Kickback Statute.

To qualify for a safe harbor under AKS, the physician must be newly practicing or relocating to an underserved, Health Profession Shortage Area (HPSA) for their specialty. Safe Harbor provisions under AKS can be difficult to meet, but they are not mandatory. This means that just because an arrangement does not meet this Safe Harbor, it does not mean it violates AKS. To meet this, Safe Harbor agreements must meet the following standards:

Anti-Kickback Statute (AKS) Safe Harbor provision for Relocation Agreements[123]

1. The agreement is written, signed by both parties, specifying benefits provided by recruiting entity, terms under which the benefits will be provided and the obligations of each party;
2. If the practitioner is leaving an established practice, at least 75% of revenues must come from new patients;
3. Relocation benefits can be paid for no more than three years, and may not be renegotiated within that time;
4. The physician cannot be required to refer to the hiring agency;
5. The physician cannot be restricted from establishing privileges at another hospital or referring to another entity;
6. The amount of benefits provided cannot vary with the volume or value of referrals generated;
7. The physician must treat Medicare and Medicaid Patients;
8. At least 75% of revenues generated are from patients in the underserved areas; and
9. Payment may not directly or indirectly benefit any person or entity in a position to influence referrals.

21. Ownership and Partnership Agreements

The opportunity to share in the ownership of a practice is enticing for a lot of physicians. Ownership represents a chance to take part in the business operations and management of the practice while sharing in revenue. When a physician joins a practice or group as an owner, they become a partner or shareholder and should sign an agreement evidencing their status. The agreements can vary in length and complexity but should contain some key elements discussed in this chapter. It is common for first drafts of such agreements to be poorly structured, particularly in smaller groups. A group of physicians may be excited about taking on a new partner or shareholder, but it is important for the paperwork to also be complete. For all of these reasons, it is advisable to have a potential shareholder or partnership agreement formally reviewed by an attorney.

Shareholder and Ownership Agreements

A shareholder agreement is a governing document through which a physician buys an ownership interest in a practice or group. It sets forth the rights and obligations of the physician as an owner.[124] Details in the agreements should include decision-making authority, control, and management; committees and voting; protective mechanisms for minority and majority owners including veto rights; and procedures for transferability and repurchase of ownership shares. Repurchase options often cover what is allowable on termination of employment, voluntary transfer, retirement, relocation from the practice's service area, death or disability, and other events requiring the practice to repurchase an ownership interest. Non-competition agreements, even if unenforceable in most contracts by state law, may be valid as part of a shareholder or ownership agreement where the physician is gaining a significant ownership stake.

How does one "Buy-In" to a practice or partnership?

A "buy-in" is generally accomplished by paying a lump sum to the practice, having deductions taken from net earnings for a few years to equal a lump sum, or paying a percentage of productivity earnings over a specified period. It is very common for a physician to be employed by a practice for a few years before he/she is offered the option to "buy-in." Ideally, during the employment phase, the physician will not be required to pay any sort of buy-in amount. Unfortunately, it is not uncommon for an employer to request that an employee pay a buy-in, even without the guarantee of becoming a full equal shareholder in the future. If the contract is not specific in this area, a physician can be employed indefinitely or terminated when an initial contract term ends and never receive any benefits from those payments. A careful review of "buy-in" provisions is crucial.

Equity versus Non-Equity in Shareholder Agreements

Medical practices and other professional practices often have an equity track and a non-equity track. An equity track is an ownership track where a physician works their way toward becoming a full shareholder and part owner of the practice. On a non-equity track, a physician will remain a regular employee indefinitely but may gain some seniority and benefits over time. A physician on a non-equity track should not be paying any portion of their productivity or net earnings toward shares in the group as part of a "buy-in." Depending on the structure of the finances of the group, a non-equity track physician may pay a percentage of productivity or have a set amount deducted from their salary for overhead expenses each pay period. It is important to thoroughly understand the finances of each individual group and practice as payment and accounting methods vary significantly.

Becoming a Partner in a General Partnership

A partnership is an agreement between two or more parties to accomplish a common goal.[125] Profits and risks are shared and allocated among the partners, and a partnership agreement is drafted as evidence of the agreed upon terms. When a practice is formed as a general partnership, each physician member is usually individually incorporated as a single member PC or LLC depending on the applicable state law. When a physician buys-in to the practice they are either purchasing a percentage of interest or a percentage of assets of the general partnership. The partnership agreement should include specific formulas for the division of expenses and profits for each partner.

Becoming a "Partner" in a Professional Corporation

As alluded to above, state law determines the way a medical practice is incorporated. In some states, medical practices and groups are incorporated as a PC, and in others, they are regular corporations or even LLCs. If the medical practice is incorporated, becoming a "partner" in a practice will mean "buying-in" to the practice by purchasing corporate shares. This means that the new "partner" will not sign a traditional partnership agreement, but instead, a shareholder agreement that is inclusive of partnership terms. There are some circumstances under which a partnership agreement may also be present if the agreement among physicians extends beyond a single professional corporation. For example, if the physicians own a surgery or dialysis center together that is not under the same corporate umbrella as the practice, there would likely be an overarching partnership agreement for all ventures.

If each shareholder must be employed by the professional corporation, again depending on state law, there should also be an employment agreement for each physician. In this case, the shareholder agreement provides details of the buy-in, percentage of ownership, repurchase agreement, calculation of overhead, voting and management rights, etc. An employment agreement contains basic terms such as work hours, vacation time, retirement plans, and obligations to the corporation and fellow physicians. All of this information can be contained in one agreement, but generally, it is separated into at least two. I have seen many situations where old employment contracts have expired, and the only contract being contemplated for signature is about purchasing shares. Though the new agreement is important; an employment agreement should also remain in place.

Important Considerations

Is there a buy-in period? If yes, for how long and how much money or what percentage of productivity?

These details should be spelled out in a contract, especially if a physician is asked to forfeit a percentage of productivity until they become a full shareholder.

What percentage of new hires make it to owner/partner status?

This is a very important question to avoid ending up in a dead-end situation where the physician has been paying in and will never receive an offer to become a full shareholder.

What are the chances the physician-owned group will be bought by a corporation or another medical group?

The current trend in the health care industry is toward consolidation.[126] Many independent groups are being acquired by large health systems or consolidating with other groups. It is always a good idea for a physician to ask this question to make sure that no current purchases are contemplated to help make an informed decision about a position. It is not uncommon for a physician to begin buying into a physician-owned practice and have that practice purchased by a large corporate entity. A physician may sign a 5-year shareholder agreement only to have the practice bought out within a few years. The physician may then be asked by the new owners to sign a new, likely more restrictive, employment agreement without the possibility of ownership. When this happens, the physician's rights as a shareholder or future partner can change dramatically, and they may find themselves bound in an employment situation where they are unhappy.

Distribution of Practice Income

A corporation or partnership can determine different methods for distributing income to shareholders. Some agreements equally divide profits by percentage of ownership, and others use formulas to determine the pay structure for each partner. One must gain a clear understanding of accounting and how all partners are paid in a practice. Senior partners can be compensated in different ways, if agreed upon, especially for administrative duties, but those methods should not be indefinite or hidden from other shareholders. It would be ideal to agree to a phase-out of any special compensation arrangements at a future date.

Management Decisions and Voting

Voting rights can be rationed to a percentage of shares and time as a shareholder or partner. Management decisions can default to senior partners in the short term, but when a physician reaches an equal ownership status, they should be given the option of involvement in management decisions. If the senior partners or shareholders do not allow new partners and shareholders to have voting and decision-making authority at the start of a relationship, a timeline should be built into the contract to show when they will have such authority.

Non-Competition Agreements as a Shareholder or Partner

Ownership of significant shares in a business can be an exception to the public policy against non-competition agreements in states such as California that favor open competition. This means that a non-compete may be enforceable in a shareholder employment agreement where it wouldn't be in a regular employment contract.[127] While it is unclear exactly how much of an ownership stake an individual would need for a non-compete to become enforceable, it is clear in California that a de minimis amount, such as one percent share ownership would not be enough, but there is no a hard line.[128] In many states, non-competes are routinely included in shareholder agreements and enforceable depending on state law.

22. Medical Directorships

Medical directorships are a way for physicians to provide oversight, leadership, and quality assurance for a medical practice, clinic, hospital, ambulance company, skilled nursing homes, etc. Medical directors are often charged with running Quality Improvement (QI) programs as well as developing medical protocol.[129] Some physicians enter into agreements as medical directors as a side job to make extra money. A lot of small organizations need physicians to be available for questions and to sign off on procedures and decisions requiring a physician's approval. These positions have been seen by some as a way to make easy money. Until recently, there has not been a lot of oversight on medical directorships, and regulators seemed to look the other way for Fair Market Value determinations.[130]

In June 2015, the Office of Inspector General (OIG) issued a fraud alert aimed at physicians contracting in general but specifically mentioned medical directors.[131] Whereas for the past few decades, fraud actions were mostly undertaken against institutions and large groups, the alert put physicians on notice that fraud regulators would be shining the spotlight directly on them and scrutinizing their contracts where necessary.

The alert says, "Physicians who enter into compensation arrangements such as medical directorships must ensure that those arrangements reflect Fair Market Value for bona fide services the physicians actually provide. Although many compensation arrangements are legitimate, a compensation arrangement may violate the anti-kickback statute if even one purpose of the arrangement is to compensate a physician for his or her past or future referrals of Federal health care program business. OIG encourages physicians to carefully consider the terms and conditions of medical directorships and other compensation arrangements before entering into them."[132]

This is a time to be extra cautious when contracting in general but especially in positions that are a little more nebulous such as medical directorships. As the final sentence of the alert says, "Those who commit fraud involving Federal health care programs are subject to possible criminal, civil, and administrative sanctions." Over the last few years, this has proven to be true as many individual physicians have been charged with fraudulent behavior for accepting payments over Fair Market Value, payments for referrals to federal health care programs, and not providing the services called for under their medical directorship agreements.[133]

Guidelines

A physician's responsibilities listed in a medical directorship contract must be the actual duties performed for the organization, and the compensation must directly reflect the work performed. To protect themselves, physicians should regularly take part in management meetings and policy discussions relating to the quality of medical care provided by the company. They should also fully understand the internal management of the organization and the expectations and reality of patient care. As the medical director, the physician's name will be tied to the organization. Therefore, it is in a physician's best interest to take an active and make sure everything is running smoothly and above board.

Areas often lacking in a medical directorship agreement include details of the compensation, work expectations, insurance coverage, and indemnification clauses.

Compensation

In light of recent crackdowns on medical director positions, the compensation arrangements in medical director contracts are often insufficient. The specific services the physician will provide each month and how the compensation correlates with those services should be clearly stated in the contract.

If the agreement is for periodic part-time services and not a full-time position, to comply with Anti- Kickback Statute and Stark Law, the hours worked, how those hours are determined, and pay per hour must be stated in the contract.[134]

If the physician is employed and paid a part-time monthly salary, time sheets or records of time worked should be kept to verify that the physician is reasonably compensated for their work. The timesheet should be submitted to an executive at the company every month. This procedure is for the protection of the physician if their status as an employee or compensation is ever questioned. If the hours are not clearly tracked for a position such as this, there is no way to prove payments were not accepted for fraudulent purposes. This is the safest way to handle proper compensation under these circumstances.

Anti-Fraud Considerations for Medical Directors

There are very important anti-fraud considerations when looking at a medical directorship agreement; the agreement must be Fair Market Value and commercially reasonable.

Fair Market Value (FMV)

Under the FMV Standard, the aggregate compensation paid to a physician over the term of the agreement must be set in advance, consistent with FMV in an arms-length transaction, and not determined in a manner that takes into account the volume or value of any referrals or business otherwise generated by the parties.[135] FMV for medical directorships is generally considered about the 50th percentile of what physicians in similar positions are making in their area and specialty though the numbers can be off as discussed in the "Fair Market Value" chapter. The only way to know if the compensation is FMV for the position is to hire an independent valuation consultant to run the numbers and compare the pay and responsibilities to that of other similarly situated physicians according to industry benchmarks. If one ever feels that they are being compensated more than they should for a position or being compensated extra for work that does not need to be done by a physician, the should look at the situation skeptically and determine if there is any possible fraud with regard to the extra payments.

Commercial Reasonableness

Under the Commercial Reasonableness standard, the employment situation is examined to see if a medical director is needed for the company and if the physician is the only medical director.[136] If a medical director is not needed for the type of work being performed, then it is not reasonable to staff a medical director. If there is already one medical director and two are not needed, it would not be reasonable to hire a second medical director. In other words, the arrangement must be a sensible, prudent business arrangement to be valid even in the absence of any kind of fraudulent activity. If a physician is needed to perform administrative medical tasks that a physician of his/her training would be equipped to handle assuming the responsibilities match the compensation each month, it should be commercially reasonable to hire that physician.

Independent Contractor Status as it applies to Medical Directorships

It is particularly important to pay close attention to the status of a medical director as an independent contractor in light of recent OIG fraud alerts. The following are merely guidelines and should not be taken as legal advice for a specific contract. To comply with many of the anti-fraud laws, an agreement should at a minimum:

1. Be in writing and signed by both parties;
2. Cover all services to be provided for the term of the agreement;
3. If the agreement is part-time rather than full time, the agreement must specify how scheduling will take place;
4. The term must not be for less than one year;

5. Compensation must be set in advance, consistent with Fair Market Value, and not take into account the volume or value of referrals or business generated between parties;
6. The agreement is not illegal in other ways; and
7. The services contracted for must be reasonable.

Bonus Arrangement

Bonus and incentive compensation arrangements must be clearly defined. Any financial arrangement that is not clearly defined is a big red flag. Some contracts contain a clause that allows the employer to determine if and when bonuses will be provided. This type of arrangement is not allowed for medical director contracts because it does not describe the bonus with sufficient certainty. A physician should not accept any payments outside of those which are specifically explained in detail in the written contract. If bonuses are not actually contemplated such a clause should be removed from the compensation agreement. If there is a possibility of a bonus, it should be defined with more detail.

Professional Liability and Other Insurance

There are four basic concerns when it comes to insurance and medical directorship agreements. First, the party procuring and paying for the insurance should be clearly identified in the contract. Sometimes, a physician and employer will discuss who will purchase insurance, but the relationship will not be accurately portrayed in the contract. It is important that it remains clear in the agreement which type of insurance is being procured and who is responsible for obtaining and paying the premium.

Sample Contract Language:

"Medical Group, Inc., shall provide professional liability insurance for Consultant as Medical Director with a policy limit of at least $1 Million per claim and with an aggregate limit of $3 Million per year at the expense of Medical Group, Inc. In the event that the policy is "claims made" Medical Group, Inc. will be responsible for obtaining professional liability tail coverage."

Second, it needs to be clear that the policy is for a medical director. Many policies have a Medical Director Exclusion. If there is an exclusion, a separate rider needs to be added to the policy. This rider covers errors and omissions made in the course of working as a medical director that are unrelated to patient care. Ask for the certificate of insurance or the whole policy if they will provide it. The certificate or policy should specifically say that a physician is covered as a medical director. If it does not, ask the insurance agent to point out the section in the whole policy that shows the medical director will be covered.

Third, it should be clear in the contract who will pay for tail insurance, if needed, after the contract has ended. Please revisit the chapter on "Insurance" for a discussion of tail insurance.

Fourth, it is a good idea for a physician as a medical director to be covered under the general liability policy of the organization for the use of equipment at work and liability issues that may arise around supervisory duties with regard to the medical staff. In addition to general liability if the physician is taking on a director or officer role in the organization, they may need separate Directors & Officers insurance (D&O) or to be included in the organizational policy.

Indemnification

Ideally, an indemnification clause should indemnify a medical director from any litigation they may face as the medical director of the organization. If someone sues the organization, he or she may very well attach the physician's name as the medical director to the lawsuit. An indemnification clause should state that the organization will assume financial responsibility associated with defending a claim or lawsuit related to the performance of duties by the medical director. Please revisit the chapter on "Indemnification" for more information on this topic.

23. Academic Medicine

Careers in academic medicine present a unique set of challenges as well as an understanding that many of the benefits of a career in academia tend to manifest over long periods. Most successful careers in academic medicine require a career plan along with evaluation and execution of that plan on a regular basis. Part One of this book discussed why it is a good idea to set goals and assess progress on those goals at regular intervals. This is particularly important in academic medicine for three reasons: First, there are usually defined criteria for promotions that need to be met by specific dates. Second, academic institutions are not generally very agile, and any changes to a physician's position or research may take months or even years to gain approval. Planning and evaluation can help make sure things continue to move forward. Third, goals of academic institutions change over time. Doctors who have defined research or career goals may need to learn skills to work within the institution's political hierarchy. There must be the political will and a consensus about how the organization wants to move forward, which can require a long-term strategy and campaign to align the institutions goals with those of the physician.

Academic Contracts, Memorandums of Understanding, and Offer Letters

Some academic institutions require physicians to sign a regular term of years contract. This is a contract for a certain number of years that contains all the provisions one might expect to be included in a contract. Other institutions may refer to a contract in a different way, for example, as a memorandum of understanding (MOU) or offer letter. It is important to understand that there are many ways to refer to a contract. An offer letter may appear to be less formal than a traditional contract in the academic medicine setting. It may only explain the basic understanding and terms of the agreement discussed between the physician and hiring parties without all of the legalese. The reason for this is that many academic institutions rely heavily on employment manuals and policies that may be referenced into an offer letter or memo. The policies, terms, and manuals are every bit as important a part of the contract as if they had been included in the hard copy of the agreement. Physicians should always make sure to review the manuals and policies referenced in their employment contracts. Key terms including termination provisions, intellectual property agreements, and restrictive covenants may be included in referenced attachments. It is important to ask for these documents if they are not provided when a physician is sent the contract.

How are academic contracts devised?

Many physicians assume since large centers in academia have legal departments, all contracts are drafted and modified by attorneys. Unfortunately, in my experience, this is most often not the case. Human Resources departments or an administrator without legal training may be the one finalizing a contract. It is of utmost importance to make sure the details of the position are included in the offer, and that those details are correct and correspond to the agreement that the physician has made with the institution. Often because of a quick drafting process or the modification of an old agreement, mistakes get made, and essential parts of the contract are left out.

Negotiation of an Academic Contract

What is negotiable in an Academic Medicine Contract? It may sound silly, but the most important thing to remember about negotiating an academic medicine contract is that they are negotiable. The informal nature of the contracts, bureaucratic structure, and collegial attitude in this setting sometimes make physicians hesitant to push for changes in their contracts. Also, many people think that academic institutions have very well-crafted contracts that are all boilerplate language and therefore cannot be changed. While there are some institutions with parts of their contracts that have been highly vetted and are unlikely to change, almost all contracts have some room for negotiation.

Some things that are possibly negotiable depending on the position and institution are compensation; sign-on and relocation bonuses; opportunity for incentive payments; moonlighting opportunities; administrative time; flexibility with certain benefits and CME time; office space, hours, and furnishings; research opportunities and funding; access to experts within the institutions (for example, biostatisticians or business students); help with research projects from medical students or residents; opportunity to take sabbatical; and student loan payment assistance.

Academic Titles and Promotions

Titles at academic institutions vary significantly. Often there are internal titles used by Human Resources for categorization purposes and external titles, such as clinical instructor, professor, director, assistant director, etc., that would be recognized as traditional titles by most people. Depending on how well structured the system is for the external titles, a physician may want to request the external or more recognizable title be added to their contract as well as business cards and marking materials.

Internal titles should be listed in contracts along with the compensation structure. Though titles do vary between different institutions, most institutions have a set rubric for advancement from clinical instructor type positions, all the way to full professors of medicine. Each step along the way has a specific number of years assigned to it along with publishing requirements for advancement. Academic advancement or a bump in status can be an area to negotiate when making a lateral transfer to a new academic institution. Physicians can sometimes change institutions and receive a full professor title much earlier in their career than if they had stayed at one institution. The process and requirements for advancement should be part of the discussion early on in the hiring process for a new academic position to maximize the possibility of a more advanced title or to lay out the requirements and expectations of all parties.

Overqualification Issues for Academic Medicine Appointments

Physicians who are mid to late career sometimes run into issues of overqualification for certain appointments at academic institutions. When a physician with a unique resume is considered for a position at an academic center, there may be a lot of red tape to hiring them simply because they do not fit the standard mold. It is counter-intuitive to think that a person would have too much experience to be on the faculty at any given academic institution, but it does happen. Whether it is a bureaucratic issue of the correct categorization of the individual within the institution, an inability to provide appropriate compensation, or a lack of fit with the current goals of the institution, these issues can sometimes put an end to a possible employment relationship.

Trusting Leadership

How much should a physician trust the promises of the department, hospital, or institutional leadership if the terms are not defined in the contract? This is a tough question to answer because it varies so much from person to person and between institutions. In my experience, there are times when verbal promises are made, and for whatever reason, a promise cannot be memorialized in a contract. Every physician has to evaluate the situation for themselves to determine their comfort level with accepting the verbal promise instead of a written promise in the contract. If it is not written down, it is not an enforceable part of the contract and may not happen. Sometimes this is a risk a physician may take when a written promise is not possible, and they trust the person making the promise.

Exclusivity Clauses and Moonlighting

Most academic institutions have an exclusivity clause in the contract for full-time employees. This means that a physician cannot work at other institutions without the approval of their employer. Please see Chapter 12 on "Restraints on Competition" for more information regarding exclusivity clauses. If there are current projects outside of the institution that the physician wishes to continue, the approval of the institution should be included as part of or as an attachment to the contract.

Sometimes there are opportunities within the same institution to moonlight or work more hours to make more money. If this is of interest to a physician applying for a position, there should be a conversation regarding possible opportunities. If there have been promises made of specific opportunities that the physician plans to undertake as part of their role either short term or long term this information can be included in the contract.

Intellectual Property Agreements in Academic Medicine

A physician will likely be asked to sign a long intellectual property agreement as part of their employment at an academic center. As stated in the chapter on Intellectual Property, these agreements are generally very inclusive and will demand ownership over most inventions and research. If a physician has their own inventions or research outside of the institution, they need to take steps to protect their own personal intellectual property from that of the institution. The best way to do this is to seek out counsel from an intellectual property attorney and possibly disclose current ownership of patents, trademarks, or copyrights at the beginning of employment.

Conclusion

Physicians should take time to plan and evaluate their careers in academia. They should also not be afraid to negotiate and ask for clarification on issues they do not understand. The collegial nature of academia should not stop a physician from advocating for themselves, obtaining a thorough understanding of their contract, or requesting the resources necessary to perform the functions of their role and job to the fullest extent possible.

Endnotes

---

[1] Contract, Cornell Law School Legal Information Institute (2017, May 31), https://www.law.cornell.edu/wex/contract.
[2] id.
[3] Boilerplate Definition, Merriam-Webster Dictionary.
[4] Independent Contractor Self Employed or Employee, IRS (n.d.), https://www.irs.gov/businesses/small-businesses-self-employed/independent-contractor-self-employed-or-employee.
[5] id.
[6] id.
[7] Cal. Corp. § 13400-13410.
[8] Partnership Agreement Definition, Black's Law Dictionary (8th Ed. 2004).
[9] Partnership Definition, Black's Law Dictionary (8th Ed. 2004).
[10] Locums Tenens Definition, Merriam-Webster Dictionary.
[11] Cal. Bus. & Prof. § 2052.
[12] Cal. Bus. & Prof. § 2400.
[13] id.
[14] id.
[15] CMS Quality Measure Development Plan: Supporting the Transition to The Quality Payment Program, Center for Medicare and Medicaid Services (June 2, 2017), https://www.cms.gov/Medicare/Quality-Initiatives-Patient-Assessment-Instruments/Value-Based-Programs/MACRA-MIPS-and-APMs/2017-CMS-MDP-Annual-Report.pdf.
[16] id.
[17] Changing how doctors get paid, Modern Healthcare (Mar. 3, 2017), http://www.modernhealthcare.com/article/20170311/MAGAZINE/303119983.
[18] Does your physician compensation exceed Fair Market Value?, Advisory.com (June 2015), https://www.advisory.com/research/medical-group-strategy-council/practice-notes/2015/june/does-your-physician-compensation-exceed-fair-market-value.
[19] 42 CFR 411.357(d)(1); 42 CFR 1001.952(d).
[20] *Boothby v. Atlas Mechanical* 6 Cal.App.4th 1595(1992).
[21] Cal. Lab. § 227.3.
[22] Independent Contractor Self Employed or Employee, IRS (n.d.), https://www.irs.gov/businesses/small-businesses-self-employed/independent-contractor-self-employed-or-employee.
[23] Social Security Act § 1877, 42 U.S.C. 1395nn; Anti-Kickback Statute 42 U.S.C. § 1320a-7b(b).
[24] Healthcare Financing Administration, 66 Fed Reg. No 3 855-965 (January 4, 2001), Codified at 42 CFR 411.

[25] Gregory Anderson, Fair Market Value: What's Fair and is it Commercially Reasonable?, American Health Lawyers Association Annual Meeting (June 2011),
https://www.healthlawyers.org/Publications/Documents/K.%20anderson.pdf.
[26] id.
[27] id.
[28] Healthcare Financing Administration, 66 Fed Reg. No 3 855-965 (January 4, 2001), Codified at 42 CFR 411.
[29] Gregory Anderson, Fair Market Value: What's Fair and is it Commercially Reasonable?, American Health Lawyers Association Annual Meeting (June 2011),
https://www.healthlawyers.org/Publications/Documents/K.%20anderson.pdf.
[30] Timothy Smith & Meghan Wong, How to Use and Not Abuse MGMA and other Survey Data in FMV Compliance Programs: Why Flawed Data Usage Leads to Increased Compliance Risk, Health Care Compliance Association (March 28, 2017), https://www.hcca-info.org/Portals/0/PDFs/Resources/Conference_Handouts/Compliance_Institute/2017/602print2.pdf.
[31] id.
[32] IRS Rev. Rul. 59-60 3.01 and Section 7.
[33] Sally Yates, Fraud Alert: Physician Compensation Arrangements May Result in Significant Liability, Office of Inspector General (June 9, 2015).
[34] Office of Public Affairs, Justice Department Recovers Over $3.7 Billion from False Claims Act Cases in Fiscal Year 2017, Department of Justice, https://www.justice.gov/opa/pr/justice-department-recovers-over-37-billion-false-claims-act-cases-fiscal-year-2017.
[35] Office of Inspector General, Medicare Fraud Strike Force, https://oig.hhs.gov/fraud/strike-force/.
[36] Employment At-Will Definition, Blacks Law Dictionary (8th Edition); Cal Lab Code §2922 (2005).
[37] Guz v. Bechtel National Inc. 24 Cal 4th 317, 336 (Cal 2000).
[38] Civil Rights Act of 1964, Title VIII 42 USC § 2000e et seq).
[39] Termination For Cause Definition, Blacks Law Dictionary (8th Edition 2004).
[40] Cure Period or Grace Period Definition, Blacks Law Dictionary (8th Ed. 2004).
[41] Breach of Contract Definition, Blacks Law Dictionary (8th Ed. 2004).
[42] Alexo, Inc. v E*Trade Group, Inc (2005) 135 CA 4th 21, 55; Weber, Lipshie & Co. v Christian (1997) 52 CA 4th 645, 653; Grail Semiconductor, Inc. v Mitsubishi Elec. & Electronics USA, Inc. (2014) 225 CA 4th 786, 800.

[43] Injunctive Relief Definition, Law.com, https://dictionary.law.com/Default.aspx?selected=963.
[44] Cal. Lab. § 227.3.
[45] Malpractice, Medical Definition, Blacks Law Dictionary (8th Edition).
[46] Medical Malpractice Insurance, American College of Physicians https://www.acponline.org/about-acp/about-internal-medicine/career-paths/residency-career-counseling/guidance/medical-malpractice-insurance.
[47] Cal. Lab. § 2802.
[48] Jacobus v. Krambo Corporation 78 Cal.App.4th 1096, 1100 (March 2000).
[49] Edwards v Arthur Andersen LLP (2008) 44 C4th 937, 945; Howard v Babcock (1993) 6 C4th 409; Application Group, Inc. v Hunter Group, Inc. (1998) 61 CA4th 881, 900.
[50] Non-Competition Agreements: Overview, Find Law, https://employment.findlaw.com/hiring-process/non-competition-agreements-overview.html.
[51] Bus & PC §16600. In re Marriage of Greaux & Mermin (2014) 223 CA4th 1242, 1249.
[52] Exclusive Agreement Definition, Blacks Law Dictionary (8th Edition, 2004).
[53] Dayton Time Lock Serv., Inc. v Silent Watchman Corp. (1975) 52 CA3d 1, 6; Comedy Club, Inc. v Improv W. Assocs. (9th Cir 2009) 553 F3d 1277, 1291; Gatsinaris v ART Corporate Solutions, Inc. (CD Cal, July 10, 2015, No. SA CV 15–0714–DOC) 2015 US Dist Lexis 90086.
[54] Cal. Lab. Code § 2863, "[a]n employee who has any business to transact on his own account, similar to that intrusted [sic] to him by his employer, shall always give the preference to the business of the employer."; Dayton Time Lock Serv. v. Silent Watchman Corp (1975) 52 CA 3d 1.
[55] Independent Contractor Definition, Blacks Law Dictionary (8th Edition).
[56] Gillian Lester, Choice of Law and Employee Restrictive Covenants: An American Perspective, 31 Comp. Lab. L. & Pol'y J. 389 (2009) https://scholarship.law.berkeley.edu/cgi/viewcontent.cgi?article=1735&context=facpubs.
[57] In re Marriage of Greaux & Mermin (2014) 223 CA 4th 1242, 1249; Edwards v. Arthur Andersen LLP (2008) 44 CA 4th 937, 945.
[58] CA Bus & P C §§ 16600-16602.5.
[59] Retirement Group v. Galante (2009) 176 CA 4th 1226; Bosley Med. Group v. Abramson (1984) 161 CA 3d 284, 288.
[60] Reeves v. Hanlon (2004) 33 C4th 1140.
[61] Loral Corp v. Moves (1985) 174 CA 3d 368, 276; SASCO v. Rosendin Elec., Inc. (2012) 207 CA 4th 837, 848.
[62] Loral Corp v. Moves (1985) 174 CA 3d 368, 276; eOnline v Chicago Consulting Partners (ND I11, March 29, 2002, No 01 C 1918) 2002 US Dist Lexis 5464.

[63] id.
[64] Rigging Int'l Mainenance Co. v. Gwin (1982) 128 CA 3d 594, 606; D'Sa v Playhut, Inc. (2000) 85 CA 4th 927, 935; Dowell v Biosense Webster, Inc (2009) 179 CA 4th 564; Edwards v. Arthur Andersen LLP (2008) 44 CA 4th 937.
[65] Terminating a patient-physician relationship, Code of Ethics Opinion 1.1.5, American Medical Association, https://www.ama-assn.org/delivering-care/ethics/terminating-patient-physician-relationship.
[66] Hill v. Medlantic Health Care Group, 933 A.2d 314 (D.C. 2007); Lee v. Dewbre, 362 S.W.2d 900 (Tex. Civ. App. Amarillo 1962) Add citation for CA: Payton v. Weaver (1982) 131Cal.App.3d 38, 45 [182 Cal.Rptr. 225]; Hongsathavij v. Queen of Angels/Hollywood Presbyterian Medical Center (1998) 62 Cal.App.4th 1123, 1138 [73 Cal.Rptr.2d695]; Thor v. Superior Court (1993) 5 Cal.4th 725, 743 [21 Cal.Rptr.2d 357, 855 P.2d 375].
[67] Grail Semiconductor, Inc. v. Mitsubishi Elec. & Electronics USA Inc. (2014) 225 CA 4th 786, 795.
[68] Pollack v. Skinsmart Dermatology & Aesthetic Center, PC [68 Pa.D. & C.4th 417 (C.P. 2004)]; Hoppens v. Haugen (Nebraska Appeals Court, 1999).
[69] Morlife, Inc. v Perry (1997) 56 CA 4th 1514, 1523.
[70] CA Bus & P C §17200; Dowell v Biosense Webster, Inc. (2009) 179 CA 4th 564, 575.
[71] Bosley Med. Group v. Abramson 161 CA 3d 284, 289 (1984).
[72] Muggill v Reuben H. Donnelley Corp. (1965) 62 c2d 239, 242; Gordon v. Termite Control v Terrones (1978) 84 CA3d 176, 178.
[73] 11.54 2 Milligram on Trade Secrets.
[74] Application Group, Inc. v. Hunter Group Inc. (1998) 61 CA 9th 881, 899; Optos Inc. v. Topcom Med Sys., Inc. (D Mass 2011) F Supp 2d 217; Pinela v. Neiman Marcus Group, Inc. (2015) 238 CA 4th 227; Verdugo v. Alliant Group, L.P. (2015) 237 CA 9th 141, 146.
[75] id.
[76] Works for Hire, US copyright Office, https://www.copyright.gov/circs/circ09.pdf.
[77] id.
[78] 8 Wash. J.L. Tech & Arts 79 (2012) WHOSE INVENTION IS IT ANYWAY? EMPLOYEE INVENTION-ASSIGNMENT AGREEMENTS AND THEIR LIMITS https://digital.law.washington.edu/dspace-law/bitstream/handle/1773.1/1169.
[79] "Alternative Dispute Resolution, Legal Information Institute, Cornell, https://www.law.cornell.edu/wex/alternative_dispute_resolution.
[80] Stephen J. Ware, Vacating Legally-Erroneous Arbitration Awards, 6 Y.B. Arb. & Mediation 56 (2014).

[81] Indemnification Clauses in Emergency Medicine Contracts March 2016 https://www.acep.org/globalassets/uploads/uploaded-files/acep/clinical-and-practice-management/resources/medical-legal/indemn-clause-ip_final_apr_2016.pdf; Pitfalls Of Hospitals Seeking Indemnity Or Contribution From Hospital Based Physicians As A Result Of "Vicarious Liability Claims" Against The Hospital, Richard Jones, Akerman Senterfitt, Tampa, FL.
https://www.americanbar.org/newsletter/publications/aba_health_esource_home/jones.html.
[82] Hold Harmless Clause Definition, Blacks Law Dictionary (8th Edition).
[83]Employer Liability for Employee Conduct
https://corporate.findlaw.com/human-resources/employer-liability-for-employee-conduct.html.
[84] Robert J. Milligan, In employment contracts, beware of agreements for indemnification - Added liability is at stake,
https://www.reliasmedia.com/articles/30872-in-employment-contracts-beware-of-agreements-for-indemnification-added-liability-is-at-stake.
[85] A Roadmap for New Physicians, OIG,
https://oig.hhs.gov/compliance/physician-education/index.asp.
[86] Safe Harbor Regulations, OIG, https://oig.hhs.gov/compliance/safe-harbor-regulations/index.asp.
[87] The Stark Truth About Stark Law, Part I, American Academy of Family Physicians, https://www.aafp.org/fpm/2003/1100/p27.html.
[88] False Claims Act (FCA), 31 U.S.C. §§3729-3733.
[89] The Three-Headed Monster of Healthcare Fraud Enforcement: The False Claims Act, Stark Law, and the Anti-Kickback Statute, American Bar Association,
https://www.americanbar.org/groups/young_lawyers/publications/tyl/topics/health-law/three-headed-monster-healthcare-fraud-enforcement-false-claims-act-stark-law-anti-kickback-statute.html.
[90] False Claims Act (FCA), 31 U.S.C. §§3729-3733.
[91] id.; https://www.thefcainsider.com/2018/03/civil-and-criminal-fraud-and-abuse-penalties-increase-and-stark-law-changes/.
[92] False Claims Act (FCA), 31 U.S.C. §§3729-3733.
[93] Kickback Definition, Dictionary.com,
https://www.dictionary.com/browse/kickback.
[94] Anti-Kickback Statute [42 U.S.C. § 1320a-7b(b)]
[95] A Roadmap for New Physicians, OIG,
https://oig.hhs.gov/compliance/physician-education/index.asp.
[96] 42 CFR 1001.952(d).
[97] 42 U.S.C. § § 1320a-7b(b)(3)(B).
[98] Stark Law FAQs, Stark Law, http://starklaw.org/stark-law-faq.htm.

[99] id.
[100] id.
[101] id.
[102] id.
[103] 42 CFR 411.357(c).
[104] 42 CFR 411.357(d).
[105] 42 CFR 411.352.
[106] A Roadmap for New Physicians, OIG, https://oig.hhs.gov/compliance/physician-education/index.asp.
[107] id.
[108] id.
[109] Sally Yates, Office of Inspector General, June 9, 2015 Fraud Alert: Physician Compensation Arrangements May Result in Significant liability.
[110] Joint Commission on Accreditation of Healthcare Organizations. Standard MS 2166. Accreditation Manual for Hospitals. 1994:66-72.
[111] AMA Guidelines for Due Process H-265.998.
[112] Joint commission https://www.jointcommission.org/.
[113] Physician Due Process Rights, Letter to Honorable Seema Verna CMS Administrator, June 11, 2018, ACEP Applauds Bill to Protect Due Process for Emergency Physicians, July 18, 2018, https://www.emra.org/be-involved/be-an-advocate/working-for-you/2018-cms-due-process/.
[114] Health Resources and Services Administration, National Practitioners Database (NPDB) https://www.npdb.hrsa.gov/helpCenter/policy.jsp; Reporting Requirements and Query Access. https://www.npdb.hrsa.gov/resources/tables/reportingQueryAccess.jsp.
[115] Q&A Reporting Clinical Privileges Actions, https://www.npdb.hrsa.gov/guidebook/EClinicalPrivilegesQA.jsp; California Medical Board, FAQs, http://www.mbc.ca.gov/Forms/Health_Facility_Reporting_FAQ.aspx.
[116] Physician Due Process Rights, Letter to Honorable Seema Verna CMS Administrator, June 11, 2018, ACEP Applauds Bill to Protect Due Process for Emergency Physicians, July 18, 2018, https://www.emra.org/be-involved/be-an-advocate/working-for-you/2018-cms-due-process/.
[117] Medically Underserved Areas and Populations, Health Resources & Services Administration, https://bhw.hrsa.gov/shortage-designation/muap.
[118] See Chapter on Fair Market Value and Anti-Fraud Laws.
[119] See Chapter on Compensation.
[120] Kim Sanger, Recruiting Physicians: Beware Stark, Anti-Kickback, and IRS Rules, https://www.hollandhart.com/recruiting-physicians.
[121] 42 CFR 1001.952(e).
[122] id.
[123] 42 CFR 1001.952(n.).

[124] Shareholder Agreement Definition,
https://thelawdictionary.org/shareholder-agreement.
[125] Partnership Definition, https://thelawdictionary.org/partnership.
[126] How Consolidation is Reshaping Health Care, Healthcare Financial Management Association, Elizabeth Barker,
http://www.hfma.org/Leadership/E-Bulletins/2017/April/How_Consolidation_Is_Reshaping_Health_Care/.
[127] CA Bus & P C §§16601-16602.5.
[128] Bosley Med. Group v Abramson (1984) 161 CA3d 284, 289.
[129] Functions of a Medical Director in a Healthcare Institutions, A Master or a Servant, https://www.ncbi.nlm.nih.gov/pmc/articles/PMC4089725/. Kossaify, A., Rasputin, B., & Lahoud, J. C. (2013). The Function of a Medical Director in Healthcare Institutions: A Master or a Servant. Health Services Insights, 6, 105–110. http://doi.org/10.4137/HSI.S13000.
[130] Easy Money as a Medical Director, Careful Feds Say, Robert Lowes, June 10, 2015, https://www.medscape.com/viewarticle/846233
[131] Sally Yates, Office of Inspector General, June 9, 2015 Fraud Alert: Physician Compensation Arrangements May Result in Significant liability. https://oig.hhs.gov/compliance/alerts/guidance/Fraud_Alert_Physician_Compensation_06092015.pdf.
[132] id.
[133] Criminal and Civil Enforcement, Office of Inspector General, https://oig.hhs.gov/fraud/enforcement/criminal/.
[134] Under the Microscope: OIG's Alert signals continued focus on physician liability, Dykema Gossett PLLC June 16, 2015, Jonathan S. Feld and Eric S. Klein from Lexology. AHLA; Fair Market Value Documentation, Robert A. Wade, Kerieg Devault, https://www.hcca-info.org/Portals/0/PDFs/Resources/Conference_Handouts/Compliance_Institute/2011/206%20Wade-2.pdf.
[135] Medical Director Agreements - What you don't document could hurt you, Kristina M. Wesch, Ferrell Fritz,
https://www.nyhealthlawblog.com/2018/07/16/medical-director-agreements-what-you-dont-document-could-hurt-you.
[136] How to evaluate commercial reasonableness in Physician Pay, Advisory Board, August 11, 2016, https://www.advisory.com/research/medical-group-strategy-council/practice-notes/2016/08/sw-commercial-reasonableness-physician-pay.

Abbreviations

ADR	Alternative Dispute Resolution
AKS	Anti-Kickback Statute
AMGA	American Medical Group Association
APC	Advanced Practice Clinicians
CEO	Chief Executive Officer
CME	Continuing Medical Education
DEA	Drug Enforcement Administration
DHS	Designated Health Services
D&O	Director and Officer Insurance
E&O	Errors and Omissions Insurance
ER	Emergency Room
FCA	False Claims Act
FMV	Fair Market Value
HPSA	Health Practitioner Shortage Area
IC	Independent Contractor
IP	Intellectual Property
LLC	Limited Liability Company
LOU	Letter of Understanding
MACRA	Medicare Access and Reauthorization Act
MIPS	Merit-Based Incentive Payment Systems
MGMA	Medical Group Management Association
MOU	Memorandum of Understanding
MUA	Medically Underserved Area
MUP	Medically Underserved Population
NDA	Non-Disclosure Agreement
OIG	Office of Inspector General
PC	Professional Corporation
PCP	Primary Care Physician
PTO	Paid Time Off
RVU	Relative Value Unit
QI	Quality Improvement

Index

G

H

I

L

M

N

O

P

Q

R

S

T

U

W

Made in the USA
Columbia, SC
11 May 2023

16435891R00100